Andrew Fagan is Deputy Director of the Human Rights Centre at the University of Essex. He is editor of the Essex Internet Encyclopedia of Human Rights and the author of many books, including *Human Rights: Confronting Myths and Misunderstandings* and (with Janet Dine) *Human Rights and Capitalism: A Multidisciplinary Perspective on Globalisation*.

In the same series:

"Unique and uniquely beautiful. . . . A single map here tells us more about the world today than a dozen abstracts or scholarly tomes." *Los Angeles Times*

"A striking new approach to cartography. . . . No one wishing to keep a grip on the reality of the world should be without these books." *International Herald Tribune*

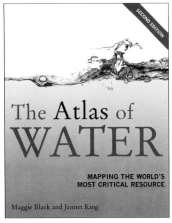

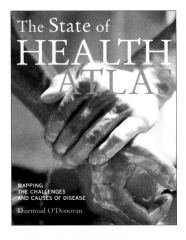

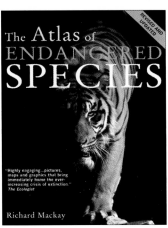

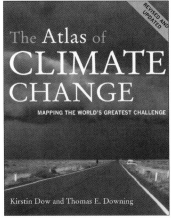

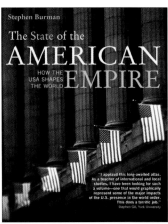

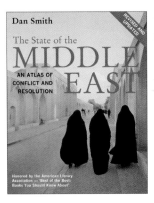

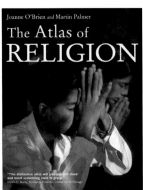

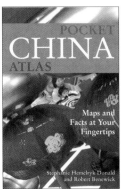

THE ATLAS OF
HUMAN
RIGHTS

Mapping Violations of Freedom Around the Globe

Andrew Fagan

UNIVERSITY OF CALIFORNIA PRESS

Berkeley   Los Angeles

University of California Press, one of the most distinguished university presses in the United States, enriches lives around the world by advancing scholarship in the humanities, social sciences, and natural sciences. Its activities are supported by the UC Press Foundation and by philanthropic contributions from individuals and institutions. For more information, visit www.ucpress.edu.

University of California Press
Berkeley and Los Angeles, California

Copyright © Myriad Editions Limited 2010

Library of Congress Control Number: 2009940428

ISBN: 978-0-520-26122-8 (cloth : alk. paper)
ISBN: 978-0-520-26123-5 (pbk. : alk. paper)

Produced for University of California Press by
Myriad Editions
Brighton, UK
www.MyriadEditions.com

Edited and co-ordinated by Jannet King and Candida Lacey
Designed by Isabelle Lewis and Corinne Pearlman
Maps and graphics created by Isabelle Lewis

Printed on paper produced from sustainable sources.
Printed and bound in Hong Kong through Lion Production
under the supervision of Bob Cassels, The Hanway Press, London.

15   14   13   12   11   10
10   9   8   7   6   5   4   3   2   1

Contents

Part 1

STATE, IDENTITY & CITIZENSHIP   16

Political Rights   18
Genuine democracy entails civil and political rights protected by an independent judiciary capable of holding the government to account.

Citizenship   20
The opportunity to vote is fundamental to the enjoyment of citizenship rights.

Wealth & Inequality   22
Nearly half the world's population continue to suffer from the effects of severe poverty.

Quality of Life   24
Quality of life is based on a range of economic and social rights consistent with leading a dignified life.

Health   26
A right to health imposes an obligation on states to promote the conditions under which all citizens can enjoy physical and mental health.

Part 2

JUDICIAL VIOLATIONS & LEGAL RESTRICTIONS   28

Torture   30
Although expressly forbidden in all circumstances, torture remains widespread.

Arbitrary Detention   32
Some states use unfair and arbitrary detention as a means of political control.

Capital Punishment   34
Punishment by death is a long-established feature of many religious traditions, and also unites otherwise quite different societies, such as the USA and China.

Policing   36
Governments have a fundamental duty to protect the security of their citizens, but far too often police officers become violators, rather than protectors, of citizens' human rights.

Part 3

FREEDOM OF EXPRESSION & CENSORSHIP   38

Freedom of Speech   40
The expression of opinions and views is widely considered a fundamental attribute of individual freedom.

Communications Censorship   42
The capacity to seek, receive and impart information is central to the exercise of individual liberty, and is an essential attribute of a genuinely open society.

Assembly & Association   44
Restrictions on the right to assemble remain a central tool by which notional "democracies" and overtly authoritarian regimes thwart and distort the will of the people.

Foreword

The abuse of the rights and freedoms of individuals is becoming more visible, and global awareness of human rights ever more focused. More is known of extreme human rights abuses, and some of the most repressive regimes have been overthrown in recent years. Many of us now live in democracies and, in theory at least, are free to enjoy the protection afforded by the ratification of various crucial human rights conventions

Despite this progress, we are still living in an era when politicians (and the media) often conflate the term "security" with "military defence" or with the secret fruits of espionage. This tends to arise because the politician is focused on the next possible threat, and on interposing barriers intended to prevent potential perpetrators from acting: a dozen men get locked up in Belmarsh, or a "Prevent" strategy targets any Muslim who talks about jihad. Or, if we are American, we lock 779 people in Guantánamo Bay beyond the rule of law, abuse prisoners in Bagram and Abu Ghraib, or render people to Egypt or Morocco so that medieval interrogation methods can extract their "intelligence" faster.

With their eyes set firmly on such hypothetical future crimes, the politicians miss the broader picture: their duty to make society safer overall. Illiberal policies rarely achieve their intended goals to any meaningful extent. Indeed, reactionary stratagems are often fated to inflame the target community, angering many who might otherwise have remained on the sidelines, and draining away the reservoir of goodwill created by such mass criminality as occurred on September 11, 2001. As one CIA agent said in 2004, for every prisoner held in Guantánamo, we have inspired or provoked another ten people to try to harm us. (Several years on, he would doubtless revise his figure upwards.) All in all, it made society – both within America and without – dramatically less safe.

So how can a responsible politician – or journalist – create a more secure society? Once we accept that dissolving our liberties is manifestly counterproductive, we can begin searching for other solutions. We must accept, however, that the purpose of the law is primarily to defend those most in need of defence. While this clearly includes children, who are both physically and mentally vulnerable, it also includes vulnerable adults who may also be despised by the majority. They might be Muslims in Guantánamo Bay in 2002. They might be Uighurs in China today. They might be asylum seekers in Australia. Or, more controversially, they might be paedophiles in the UK and USA. The word "prejudice" comes, of course, from the Latin root meaning pre-judgement, reaching a conclusion without being troubled by the facts. The purpose of human rights is to ensure that we view everyone who is the object of such prejudice as a human being, and prevent majoritarian populism from trampling on them. This should be a central object of government, for when a government behaves decently it maximizes the chance of our establishing a decent society.

This book is a timely reminder of the issues at stake. As globalization becomes a byword in the world of capitalism, so it is in the world of human rights. And the very term is telling: While constitutional or legal rights may be limited to a particular group, or while nations may show an interest only in their own citizens, human rights are self-evidently for all people. The human rights movement – in marches, petitions, campaigns, blogging, and much more besides – has unleashed an energy for change that cannot be underestimated. Aung San Suu Kyi's name has become synonymous with the campaign for democracy in Burma; Shirin Ebadi's with campaigning for women's equality in Iran; the campaign for the abolition of the death penalty goes from strength to strength. One of the rewards of the kind of mapping used in this atlas is that the reader is encouraged to think about countries that perhaps have not recently figured in the headlines, and to draw some unexpected conclusions by comparing countries from different regions. Many readers will be surprised, for instance, to see how often the USA and Iran are in the same political category.

We can never be complacent. Despite the ratification by over 145 states of the Convention Against Torture, it remains widespread, with cases documented from Azerbaijan to Brazil, Eritrea to Moldova. And even though the family of civilized nations appears uniform in rejecting torture, the first decade of the 21st century saw the USA resorting to what George Bush referred to euphemistically as "enhanced interrogation techniques", but which the Spanish Inquisition was more honest in describing as *tortura del agua* – waterboarding.

The pattern over the past 50 years has been of an ever-expanding pool of fundamental human rights, which now includes the right to the highest attainable standard of physical and mental health, and to a basic education, as well as the more accepted rights to freedom of speech, assembly and religion, and the right not to be imprisoned without trial, or to be tortured. All our futures are bound up with the upholding of human rights, not just in our own countries but in countries elsewhere in the world, and this book is a welcome resource for anyone seeking to understand the momentous changes taking place and the challenges that remain.

Clive Stafford Smith
Director, Reprieve
www.reprieve.org.uk

Acknowledgements

I owe a deep sense of gratitude to a number of people. Working with Myriad has been an absolute delight and I applaud the work of everyone there. A special word of thanks is due to Candida Lacey, who initially persuaded me of the merits and appeal of this volume. I am deeply grateful to her for having given me this opportunity. Jannet King has proven to be a wonderful editor. Her professionalism, rigour, and sheer enthusiasm has greatly improved the quality of this atlas. She patiently guided me through the earlier stages of work whose format and approach was mostly unfamiliar to me. A special mention must also be made of the precociously talented Eve Lacey, who devised the initial outline and contents of this volume. It is a testament to her that the end product differs hardly at all from her initial vision.

I continue to benefit from my association with one of the world's leading academic human rights centres and the expertise to be found at the University of Essex. Particular mention is due to Kevin Boyle, Edzia Carvalho, Geoff Gilbert, Todd Landman, and Sheldon Leader, all of whom offered invaluable advice and insight. Ryan Hill made an invaluable contribution to assembling data and research for extensive parts of this volume. Amongst Ryan's many talents can be added that of an exemplary researcher. Christina Szurlej also provided much needed data and research and I am grateful to her for her contribution.

Finally, I must thank my partner Julia for everything, not least of which her patience and understanding during those periods of my mental absence in thinking about and producing this work.

Andrew Fagan

Introduction

Over 60 years have passed since the publication of the Universal Declaration of Human Rights (UDHR). It constituted then and remains now the most significant landmark in the development of the modern human rights movement. Its authors sought to draw an unequivocal moral line in the sand between humankind's capacity to perpetrate acts of gross and systematic inhumanity and our potential to identify and comply with the basic conditions for exercising and realizing our humanity. The eventual fruit of this labour was 30 separate articles, which, taken together, identify and stipulate areas of human existence worthy of fundamental protection, ranging from a right to be free from torture to a right to receive social security. The UDHR also affirms fundamental rights to such things as, for example, a right to a fair legal hearing, rights to participate in the political affairs of one's community, rights to freedom of religion and conscience, a right to marry the person of one's choosing, a right to receive free primary education, rights to adequate material provision and sustenance, and even a right to participate in the cultural practices of one's community. In essence, it aims to establish a set of moral guarantees for protecting each individual human being's fundamental dignity and moral worth, and may be thought of as formulating the qualities of humanity. It is a document whose principal motivation is to prevent and forestall any further acts of systematic inhumanity.

> The UDHR aims to establish a set of moral guarantees for protecting each individual human being's fundamental dignity and moral worth.

Since the publication of the UDHR there has been an exponential growth in what has become a global human rights infrastructure. The most recognizable manifestation of this development can be found in the establishment of an international body of human rights law. Taking the UDHR as their principal foundation-stone, international human rights covenants, treaties, conventions, protocols, and instruments now cover a comprehensive expanse of human activities. International human rights law is concerned with protecting and promoting an individual's human rights through the creation and imposition of duties, and obligations to both refrain from those actions and conditions which undermine human rights, and to actively establish and protect those actions and conditions considered to be prerequisite for the enjoyment of human rights. Human rights are characteristically said to correlate with corresponding duties.

While individual human beings are the intended ultimate beneficiaries of the protection and promotion of human rights, the onus to establish the conditions necessary for realizing this end typically fall upon nation-states. There are historical and practical justifications for this arrangement. The UDHR was a response to the atrocities committed by nation-states during the first half of the 20th century, in particular, Nazi Germany's perpetration of the Holocaust. Practically, the nation-state is considered not just to be the most likely violator of human rights but also the agent best placed to protect and promote human rights, both through its own unilateral actions and resources, and through multilateral action with other states. The vast majority of the world's sovereign nation-states have recognized, to varying extents, human rights as an international body of law.

Beyond national frontiers
The legal codification of the moral spirit of the UDHR does not exhaust human rights as a global phenomenon. Beyond the strictly legal realm, human rights have also established a degree of recognition and authority within the civil and political spheres. While less overtly and comprehensively "global" than its legal counterpart, the civil and political domain of human rights comprises organizations, political

parties, networks and individuals committed to protecting and promoting human rights where no human rights law exists or where international human rights law may have been ratified but is yet to be implemented. Indeed, to a certain extent, one may think of this domain of human rights as motivated by the limitations of human rights law. It is, after all, comparatively easy for a nation-state to ratify some aspect of international human rights law; actively implementing any such ratification requires going beyond affirming merely nice-sounding gestures and pronouncements, however. Human rights defenders within the civil and political spheres characteristically aim to raise awareness of practices and conditions that violate the terms of a recognized human rights law, or to testify to instances where no such law has yet been established. Through campaigning and lobbying, these human rights defenders ultimately aim to overcome human rights abuse through the use of politics and the concerted actions of civil society.

The civil and political sphere of the human rights infrastructure does extend beyond national frontiers, as is most apparent in the work of organizations such as Amnesty International and Human Rights Watch, which aim to confront human rights abuses in both the developed and the developing world. It would, however, be fair to say that this sphere is most developed within established liberal-democratic societies. As the subsequent data and analysis of this atlas will demonstrate, all states violate human rights. Some states do so occasionally and exceptionally; other states do so systematically and concertedly. Some human rights organizations and defenders are to be found within the latter category of states; many more exist within the former. The distinction can, no doubt, be accounted for in part by reference to the differential risks and obstacles human rights defenders are confronted by in the pursuit of their civil and political goals. For some, seeking to defend human rights really is a matter of life and death.

Human rights have become a global phenomenon. As a result, the language of human rights is now a central element of many people's campaigns for justice. Indeed, for many, human rights are now considered to be synonymous with legal, political, social and even economic justice. Human rights appear to offer the means by which we may seek to overcome oppression and discrimination irrespective of nationality, class, creed, gender, ethnicity, or even ideological commitment. In belonging to all human beings simply by virtue of being human, human rights offer the promise of overcoming the partial barriers and boundaries which otherwise divide us. However, while the rhetoric of human rights is manifestly robust, attempts to disclose and identify the fundamental justifications for a commitment to human rights raise some interesting issues and questions.

> Human rights have become a global phenomenon.

Justifying a human right

Few would seek to question the immorality of genocide or torture. Similarly, most people would agree that the taking of innocent human life can never ultimately be justified. Most would agree that human rights are justified as a means to protect human beings against such wrongs. In these cases there seems little need for further justification. However, this appeal to a basic moral intuition will not extend to provide similarly secure grounds for a commitment to all the human rights enshrined within the UDHR. Not everyone agrees that they and every other human being should enjoy human rights against, for example, racism and sexism. What some of us may perceive to be nothing more than unjustifiable forms of discrimination and inequality, others will defend as integral features of their religious or cultural traditions, beliefs, and practices. Likewise, practices which some may consider thoroughly justified manifestations of artistic freedom or freedom of conscience, may be condemned by others as morally unacceptable. Consider, for example, a dispute between those who demand censorship of a theatrical production on the grounds that it is blasphemous or fundamentally disrespectful to their beliefs, and those who view and defend the production as a legitimate form of art. An even more controversial example is evident in disputes between human rights defenders and those regimes that discriminate against women through their laws and conventions.

Justifying human rights requires determining what the ultimate basis of human rights is and how far any such right may be applied. One of the great strengths of human rights consists precisely in the common and shared moral belief system which they offer otherwise very diverse and disparate communities of human beings. However, this appeal to a shared and common understanding also raises one of the principal obstacles to any attempt to intellectually justify a commitment to human rights. Simply appealing to people's existing opinions and practices will not enable us to achieve a genuinely defensible justification of human rights. Providing such a justification remains necessary if the force of any commitment to human rights is not to be determined by what the majority happen to believe or what powerful opinion-formers have sought to represent as true. All too often, human rights campaigns are conducted by minorities, or dissidents, or the relatively powerless in the name of human values and ideals which purport to transcend more partial and limited interests. The justification of human rights requires an engagement with values and ideals. The most prominent values and ideals for the purposes of human rights are human dignity, individual liberty, and personal equality. We might refer to these as the secular trinity of the human rights corpus. Dignity, liberty, and equality are explicitly appealed to within the UDHR. They are also predominant within the arguments presented by many human rights theorists in their attempts to justify a commitment to human rights. Each of these ideals has been and remains long-standing features of many religious and morally secular world views. To this extent, human rights theorists have adopted and reassembled the moral weaponry of others in their specific attempt to account for the moral authority of human rights. Each of these ideals and values is conceptually complex and has attracted extensive analysis and discussion.

> The most prominent values and ideals for the purposes of human rights are human dignity, individual liberty, and personal equality.

Dignity, liberty, and equality

When combined within the human rights doctrine, dignity, liberty, and equality serve to ground any human being's claims to human rights and simultaneously offer a determination of the scope of any such claim. Thus, we are often said to possess human rights by virtue of our inherent dignity. Each human being has a moral standing and worth in their own right, independently from their social, political, and economic standing and achievements. Inherent dignity is a value which cannot be differentially measured or distributed: we all possess it and to the same degree. The capacity to exercise free choices is also an attribute considered by human rights theorists to be essential to human agency. We are not creatures of instinct, nor are our actions thoroughly determined by our genetic inheritance. Through the exercise of reason, we make choices over how we wish our lives to proceed.

Separate human rights articles aim to support this capacity for the exercise of choice through protecting and promoting civil and political freedoms, such as, for example, the right to vote, the right to assemble freely with others, and the right to marry (or not to marry) the spouse of one's own choosing. Other human rights aim to establish material conditions that seek to protect human beings from the systematic effects of absolute poverty, malnutrition, starvation, and chronic ill-health. Each of these fundamental human rights ultimately has its basis in a commitment to the ideal of individual liberty as a moral good and an essential feature of human agency. In founding any legal or political system on the value of individual liberty for all, it is essential to attach an equality proviso to the determination of the legitimate scope of any individual's liberty. Failure to do so may result in some people's exercise of liberty entailing the servitude or oppression of others. The equality ideal makes an indispensable contribution to the human rights doctrine through its requirement that all human beings are accorded equal moral and legal value. It goes further through the creation of rules and regulations which seek to protect and promote each individual's exercise of equal liberty.

Human rights do not justify the assertion of one person's will upon another. Nor do they entitle a political movement freedom of expression to publicize political goals based upon an overtly racist doctrine that seeks to deny the moral standing of specific ethnic or racial groups. Through combining the ideals of individual liberty and personal equality the human rights doctrine aims to delineate the legitimate scope of the exercise of individual liberty whilst simultaneously requiring each human agent to respect the claims to equal liberty of all human agents. Initially, these claims apply most forcibly to those who share the same political community, but the logic of the argument ultimately extends to cover all human beings everywhere.

> Human rights do not provide a means for individuals to assert their will upon others.

The continuing appeal and moral authority of human rights depends upon a continuing and widespread adherence to these fundamental ideals of dignity, liberty, and equality. If most human communities stopped endorsing these values and ideals, the moral force and legitimacy of human rights would be severely undermined. States continue to violate their citizens' human rights in many parts of the world: some do so as part of a concerted and deliberate policy, others do so through neglect and a lack of concern. The likelihood of other, more overtly human rights-respecting, states intervening to protect human rights is significantly affected by hard-headed calculations of national interest, which results in open hypocrisy at worst or mere inconsistency at best. In addition to states, other institutions and agents have been increasingly identified as perpetrating human rights abuses, from communities to trans-national corporations. In the face of the widespread endorsement of the spirit of human rights, wholesale abuses continue. However, the fact that they are recognized as such, and are capable of moral condemnation, is itself a consequence of the moral authority of human rights.

Criticisms of universal human rights

Some argue that the ideals of individual liberty and personal equality are not universally valid and that seeking to promote these ideals is part of a continuing attempt by "western" societies to convert the rest of the world to the values and ideals which are espoused (if not always adhered to) in liberal-democratic societies. Different human communities and societies produce and espouse different moral belief systems. There is no ultimate reason why any one such belief system should be considered legitimate for all. This line of criticism is particularly pertinent for evaluating those cultural and social practices which appear to violate the ideals of individual liberty and personal equality. The rights of women and sexual minorities are particularly problematic in this regard. Otherwise socially authoritative practices and traditions have been condemned by human rights defenders on the grounds that social conventions offer no defence for human rights abuse. In these instances, some human rights campaigns have been condemned as forms of cultural imperialism. However, we are entitled to ask who ultimately benefits from continuing forms of discrimination and inequality? A closer inspection of the lives and opinions of those condemned to a lower status within some such communities will reveal that not every member of the community is opposed to the establishment of human rights as a means, not for imposing foreign values and ideals, but for protecting otherwise vulnerable human beings.

Human rights campaigns have also attracted criticism from within the electorates of established liberal-democratic societies on several grounds. The most significant area of concern is a perception that a commitment to human rights binds the hands of governments and security forces in their attempts to prevent terrorist atrocities. Underlying this debate is an assumption that human rights are not things each human being is entitled to by virtue simply of being human, as the UDHR declares, but should be accorded to those who are willing to accept and respect the fundamental rights of all other human beings as a necessary condition of enjoying their own claims to the protection afforded by human rights. Would-be terrorists are considered to fail this test by their lack of regard for the lives of their potential victims. In some instances, the human rights-based legal restraints placed upon governments in respect of detaining suspects without charge, security forces' violation of an individual's privacy through surveillance and forms of ethnic profiling in identifying potential suspects have all enjoyed a degree of popular support in various western countries despite their implications for human rights.

It may well be, after all, an essentially human instinct to seek to protect oneself against threats to one's existence. The question is how real and widespread is the threat? More importantly, much of this debate simply avoids or overlooks the conditions out of which would-be terrorists emerge. Preventive mechanisms which ultimately perpetuate discrimination and inequality will most likely only serve to further fuel the ire of those whose experience of discrimination and inequality provides a principal, if never justifiable, motive for the actions they pursue.

Human rights should be understood as an evolving and ever-developing doctrine. It is neither cast in concrete nor a moral template for all things of moral worth. (There are many things which it is morally good to have: the love of others, esteem and recognition of one's work, the realization of one's full potential as a human being, which ought not to be considered fundamental human rights.)

> The legitimate aims of human rights are, …to eradicate forms of significant and systematic human suffering.

Human rights do not aim to create the perfect world or represent a vision of a new, secular utopia. The legitimate aims of human rights are, in fact, rather more modest: to eradicate forms of significant and systematic human suffering. A world in which all human beings enjoyed their human rights would not include many or all of the deplorable conditions that we map in the proceeding pages. It would, instead, be a world devoid of despotic rulers, of regimes which silence opposition through torture, false imprisonment and gross intimidation; a world devoid of starvation and the millions of premature deaths which result every year from lack of access to clean drinking water; a world genuinely rid of genocide and forms of ethnic cleansing. It would be a world very much better than the one we currently inhabit.

Achieving such a world is not a task restricted to the few. It does not require occupying political office, or securing a legal career. It does not require the accumulation of specialized skills or qualifications in making the world a better place. It is not, therefore, a task for someone else to perform. Genuinely achieving a truly humane world is a challenge to us all and not just the select few.

Andrew Fagan
Colchester, UK, 2009

Major Human Rights Conventions

UN Convention on the Prevention and Punishment of the Crime of Genocide, 1948

International Covenant on Civil and Political Rights, 1966

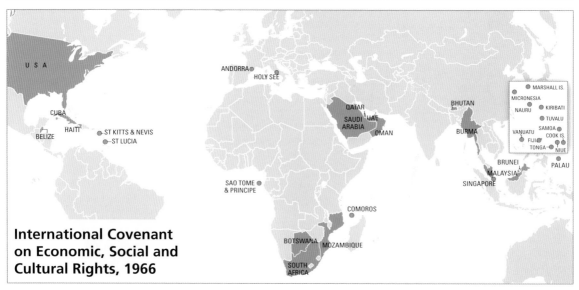

International Covenant on Economic, Social and Cultural Rights, 1966

Non-ratifying countries, September 2009

UN Convention on the Elimination of All Forms of Discrimination against Women, 1979

UN Convention against Torture and Other Cruel, Inhuman or Degrading Treatment or Punishment, 1984

UN Convention on the Rights of the Child, 1989

State, Identity & Citizenship

Freedom is a universal value and an essential element of any regime that respects human rights. In order for people to enjoy their freedom, a number of conditions are required. At the political level it is essential that societies are founded upon democratic principles, which enable people to determine how they wish to be governed and by whom.

Since the fall of the Soviet Union there has been a steady increase in notional democracies. However, simply securing democratic institutions and periodic elections may not be sufficient to prevent the abuse of political power and ensuing human rights violations. In some cases, fledgling democracies suffer from continuing corruption and the manipulation of elections. Few such elections have succeeded in changing a ruling government, despite often widespread opposition.

In more established democracies, political apathy amongst a growing number of the electorate is a cause for concern, as it raises serious questions about the accountability and representative nature of otherwise democratically elected governments.

Beyond fledgling and established democracies remain a small number of regimes that refuse to hold any elections, and continue to expose their citizens to the fundamental violation of human rights that this entails.

The opportunity to enjoy freedom is also fundamentally affected by wealth and access to material resources. Throughout the world, wealth is unequally distributed. Across much of the developing world freedom is severely restricted by crippling levels of poverty and underdevelopment, which afflict the vast majority of the populations of these countries. The severest effects of the unequal distribution of wealth and resources are apparent in the very poor quality of life, characterized by hunger, chronic ill-health, lack of basic services and premature death, experienced by those whose human rights are most threatened in this respect. For these people, the promise offered by human rights of being able to lead a genuinely free life remains a distant dream.

COLOMBIA: An elderly man prepares to vote in a presidential election.

Political Rights

Genuine democracy entails a complex array of civil and political rights, such as freedom of assembly and peaceful protest, protected by an independent judiciary capable of holding the government to account if it threatens to infringe these rights.

Democracies must also enshrine rights to non-discrimination and fundamental equality so that the losers of free and fair election are protected from political oppression by the majority party. On occasion, protecting the rights of minorities or groups traditionally discriminated against may actually prove unpopular with the electorate.

The majority of countries claim to be "democratic" to the extent that periodic elections are held to determine who holds office. However, democracy is a term open to abuse.

The right to "democracy" is not explicitly stated in any UN Convention, but is implicit in a number of articles of the International Covenant on Civil and Political Rights. From a human rights perspective, more is required than periodic elections for a democracy to be genuine. Those elections must be free, transparent, conducted on the basis of "one-person one-vote", and people must be able to cast their votes secretly, free from surveillance and intimidation.

It is widely believed that the end of the Cold War has resulted in the growth of democracies across the world. The reality is more complex. Notional democracies, which do not satisfactorily enshrine fundamental human rights, are all too often guilty of violating those rights.

What the law says...

All peoples have the right of self-determination. By virtue of that right they freely determine their political status and freely pursue their economic, social and cultural development.

International Covenant on Civil and Political Rights, 1966, Article 1

Political Systems
2009

- ■ established democracy
- ■ weak, uncertain or transitional democracy
- ■ effective or formal one-party rule
- ■ military dictatorship
- ■ monarchy or theocracy
- ■ state of disorder
- ■ dependent territory

VENEZUELA Hugo Chávez, first elected president in 1998, has survived numerous coup attempts and won three presidential elections. In 2007, a referendum narrowly rejected his proposals to extend his powers, but in 2009 voters backed his proposal to remove restrictions on the number of presidential terms.

PARAGUAY In 2008, the rule of the conservative Colorado Party was ended by Bishop Fernando Lula's presidential election victory.

True democracies are tolerant of political opposition and protest, and allow their citizens to demonstrate in support of their views.

State, Identity & Citizenship

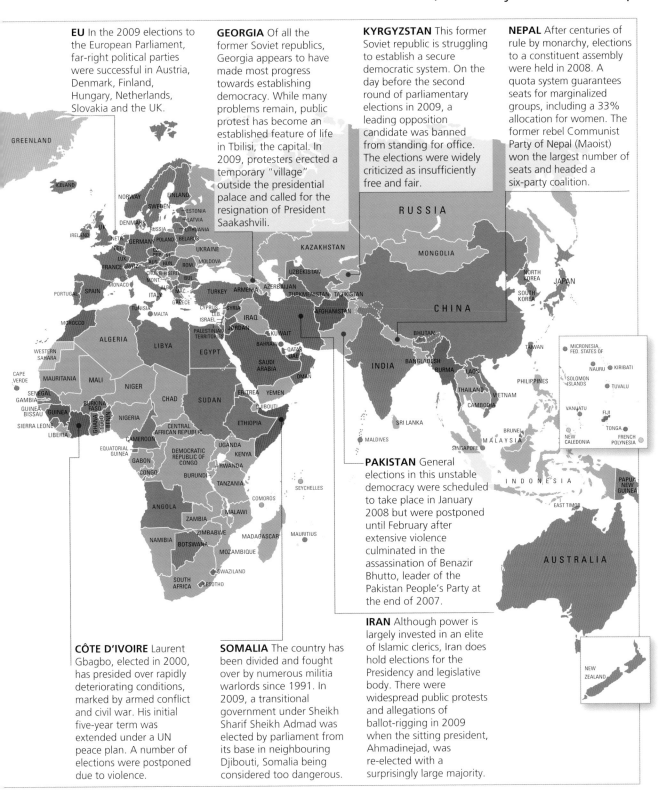

EU In the 2009 elections to the European Parliament, far-right political parties were successful in Austria, Denmark, Finland, Hungary, Netherlands, Slovakia and the UK.

GEORGIA Of all the former Soviet republics, Georgia appears to have made most progress towards establishing democracy. While many problems remain, public protest has become an established feature of life in Tbilisi, the capital. In 2009, protesters erected a temporary "village" outside the presidential palace and called for the resignation of President Saakashvili.

KYRGYZSTAN This former Soviet republic is struggling to establish a secure democratic system. On the day before the second round of parliamentary elections in 2009, a leading opposition candidate was banned from standing for office. The elections were widely criticized as insufficiently free and fair.

NEPAL After centuries of rule by monarchy, elections to a constituent assembly were held in 2008. A quota system guarantees seats for marginalized groups, including a 33% allocation for women. The former rebel Communist Party of Nepal (Maoist) won the largest number of seats and headed a six-party coalition.

CÔTE D'IVOIRE Laurent Gbagbo, elected in 2000, has presided over rapidly deteriorating conditions, marked by armed conflict and civil war. His initial five-year term was extended under a UN peace plan. A number of elections were postponed due to violence.

SOMALIA The country has been divided and fought over by numerous militia warlords since 1991. In 2009, a transitional government under Sheikh Sharif Sheikh Admad was elected by parliament from its base in neighbouring Djibouti, Somalia being considered too dangerous.

PAKISTAN General elections in this unstable democracy were scheduled to take place in January 2008 but were postponed until February after extensive violence culminated in the assassination of Benazir Bhutto, leader of the Pakistan People's Party at the end of 2007.

IRAN Although power is largely invested in an elite of Islamic clerics, Iran does hold elections for the Presidency and legislative body. There were widespread public protests and allegations of ballot-rigging in 2009 when the sitting president, Ahmadinejad, was re-elected with a surprisingly large majority.

Citizenship

The opportunity to vote is fundamental to the enjoyment of citizenship rights. Since the early 1990s, the number of people able to do so has increased markedly, largely due to the collapse of the Soviet Union and other state socialist regimes.

Despite this development, many people experience significant constraints on their freedom to vote for their elected representatives. Some potential voters are restricted on grounds of age, gender, employment in state services, being a member of the armed forces, unemployment and even marital status. Conversely, in other countries, voting is compulsory for all those registered to vote, and failure or refusal to do so can result in a criminal prosecution.

In many countries, turn-out even in important national elections remains low. Registered voters fail to exercise their right for a variety of reasons. These include a lack of interest in politics, a sense of disillusionment with politicians, and a perception that the substantive differences between candidates are negligible. Voters may also choose not to vote as a form of protest at what they consider to be unfairly run elections.

What the law says...

Every citizen shall have the right and the opportunity ... to vote and to be elected at genuine periodic elections which shall be by universal and equal suffrage and shall be held by secret ballot, guaranteeing the free expression of the will of the electors.

International Convenant on Civil and Political Rights 1966, Article 25 (b)

...**only 57%** of **Americans** voted in the 2008 **presidential election**...

Voter Turnout

In parliamentary elections
most recent available data

- 80% or more
- 70% – 79%
- 60% – 69%
- 50% – 59%
- fewer than 50%
- no data

...**33%** of people in the world are **unable** to exercise their right **to vote** in democratic elections...

Right to Vote

Restrictions on suffrage*
2009

- universal suffrage within age limitations
- universal male suffrage only
- no data
- ● military and/or police prohibited from voting
- ✖ voting compulsory within age limitations

* This is an assessment of legal right and does not reflect current political restrictions on the exercise of democracy.

Wealth & Inequality

The world is characterized by gross inequalities in wealth. In spite of vast global resources, nearly half the world's population continue to suffer from the effects of severe poverty.

Almost 3 billion people struggle to survive on or below the poverty line, which the World Bank sets at an income per person of $2 a day. Meanwhile, there are almost 800 billionaires and too many millionaires to count – a significant number of whom are to be found in those countries with large populations living in extreme poverty.

Even in times of global economic recession there are sufficient financial resources to eradicate absolute poverty, which has a devastating impact on basic human rights, depriving people of the essential means of survival, such as an adequate diet, a clean and reliable water supply, and medicine when they fall sick.

In 2000, the UN established eight Millennium Development Goals for overcoming the effects of severe poverty by the year 2015. While some progress has been made, it is widely believed that none will be fully realized by the target date. Indeed, the effects of the global economic recession have set back or even reversed the modest progress achieved in, for example, reducing the number of people living below the absolute poverty line, which increased in 2008 by an estimated 90 million people.

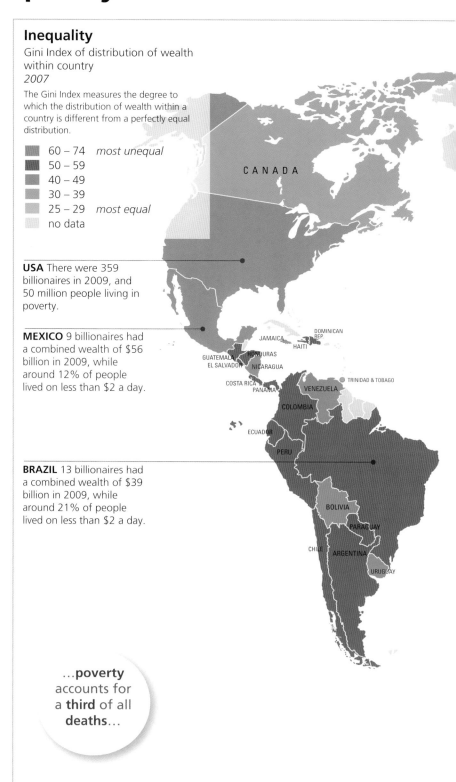

Inequality

Gini Index of distribution of wealth within country
2007

The Gini Index measures the degree to which the distribution of wealth within a country is different from a perfectly equal distribution.

- 60 – 74   *most unequal*
- 50 – 59
- 40 – 49
- 30 – 39
- 25 – 29   *most equal*
- no data

USA There were 359 billionaires in 2009, and 50 million people living in poverty.

MEXICO 9 billionaires had a combined wealth of $56 billion in 2009, while around 12% of people lived on less than $2 a day.

BRAZIL 13 billionaires had a combined wealth of $39 billion in 2009, while around 21% of people lived on less than $2 a day.

...**poverty** accounts for a **third** of all **deaths**...

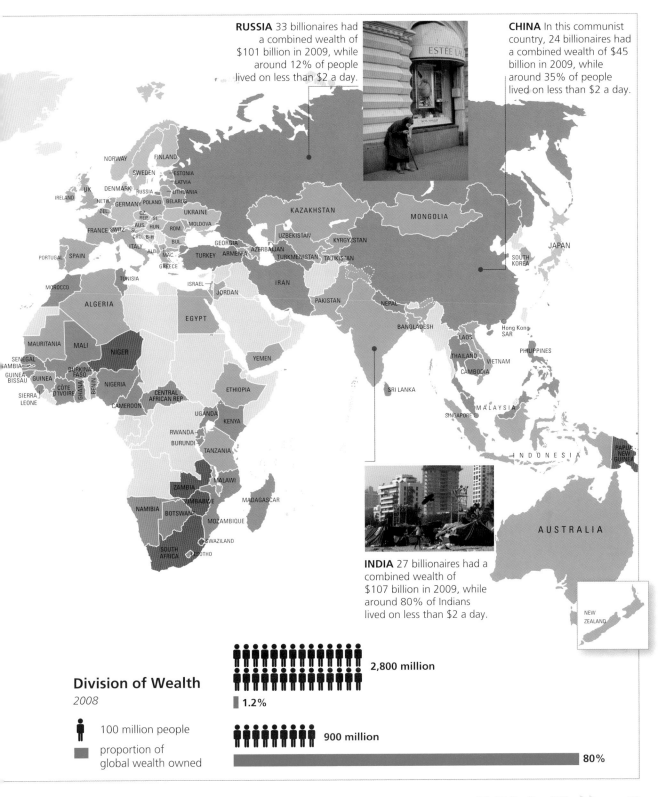

RUSSIA 33 billionaires had a combined wealth of $101 billion in 2009, while around 12% of people lived on less than $2 a day.

CHINA In this communist country, 24 billionaires had a combined wealth of $45 billion in 2009, while around 35% of people lived on less than $2 a day.

INDIA 27 billionaires had a combined wealth of $107 billion in 2009, while around 80% of Indians lived on less than $2 a day.

Division of Wealth
2008

👤 100 million people

▮ proportion of global wealth owned

2,800 million
▮ 1.2%

900 million
80%

Quality of Life

Quality of life is based on a range of economic and social rights. These include the right to an adequate diet, access to clean drinking water, and an overall level of development consistent with leading a dignified life.

While the conditions for realizing these rights depend largely on the financial resources deployed, quality of life cannot simply be equated to the size of a country's gross national income. What counts is not how much wealth a nation possesses, but what proportion is spent on enhancing the economic and social conditions of all its citizens. There are a number of states where there is wide disparity between indicators of national wealth and of quality of life.

More immediately, access to clean drinking water and levels of malnutrition provide the clearest indicators of conditions that not only adversely impact people's quality of life, but threaten their ability to remain alive. In this respect, many millions of people's fundamental human right to life is threatened each and every day.

What the law says...

The States Parties ... recognize the right of everyone to an adequate standard of living for himself and his family, including adequate food, clothing and housing, and to the continuous improvement of living conditions.

International Covenant on Economic, Social and Cultural Rights, 1976, Article 11.1

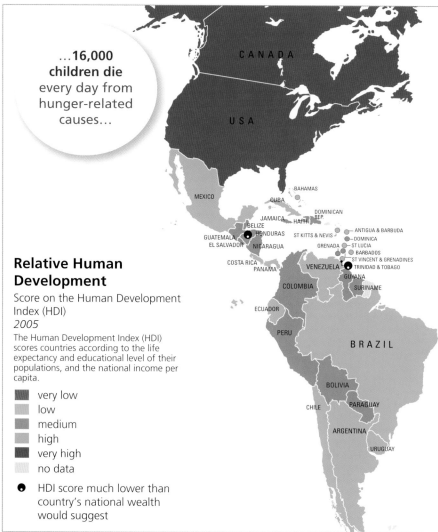

...**16,000 children die** every day from hunger-related causes...

Relative Human Development

Score on the Human Development Index (HDI)
2005

The Human Development Index (HDI) scores countries according to the life expectancy and educational level of their populations, and the national income per capita.

- very low
- low
- medium
- high
- very high
- no data

● HDI score much lower than country's national wealth would suggest

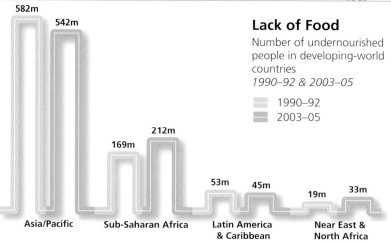

Lack of Food

Number of undernourished people in developing-world countries
1990–92 & 2003–05

- 1990–92
- 2003–05

582m 542m   Asia/Pacific
169m 212m   Sub-Saharan Africa
53m   45m   Latin America & Caribbean
19m   33m   Near East & North Africa

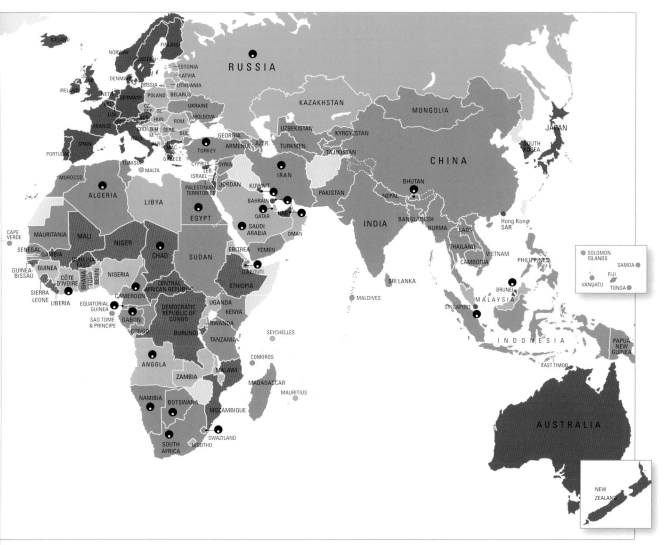

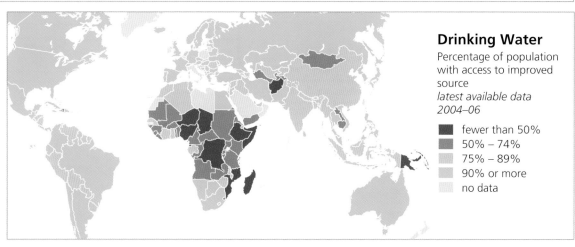

Drinking Water

Percentage of population
with access to improved
source
*latest available data
2004–06*

- fewer than 50%
- 50% – 74%
- 75% – 89%
- 90% or more
- no data

Health

A right to health imposes an obligation on states to promote the conditions under which all citizens can enjoy physical and mental health.

Full recognition of a human right to the resources necessary for a healthy life is a recent development, and most countries are now party to at least one human rights treaty that addresses health issues. Previously, some had dismissed such a claim as an unrealizable aspiration.

The opportunity to lead a healthy life extends beyond merely being free from illness and disease. States are required to strive to improve health services and the health of their populations. Wide disparities in access to services are an indication of the failure of governments to address the health rights of all their citizens. While financial resources are a significant factor, the effective implementation of policies is equally important. Improvements in health are attained by addressing a combination of rights – those to education, nutrition and a decent standard of living.

The violation of a range of human rights has an adverse impact on health. Discriminatory policies and actions can also both directly contribute to ill-health and affect the likelihood of individuals receiving adequate treatment.

The production, marketing and consumption of tobacco is an example of how a few transnational companies can adversely impact a wide range of human rights, including the use of child labour and of unsafe and unhealthy working conditions, the promotion of tobacco products to children and adults, and the failure of governments to ensure that their citizens are fully informed of the harmful effects of smoking, or protected from the risks associated with second-hand smoke.

What the law says...

The States Parties to the present Covenant recognize the right of everyone to the enjoyment of the highest attainable standard of physical and mental health.

International Covenant on Economic, Social and Cultural Rights, 1966 Article 12

Education for Life

"…mortality is inversely associated with educational attainment; that is, the average risk of death decreases markedly with increasing educational attainment."

US death rate per 100,000:
- no high-school diploma 529
- high-school diploma 465
- college degree 200

US National Vital Statistics Reports, April 2009

Links Between Human Rights and Health

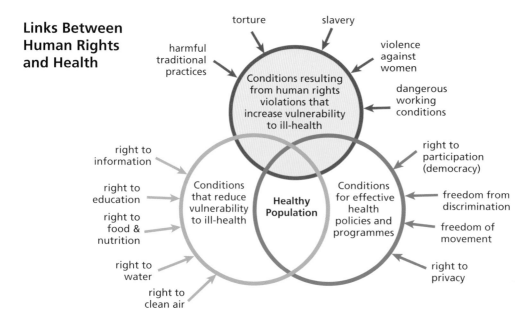

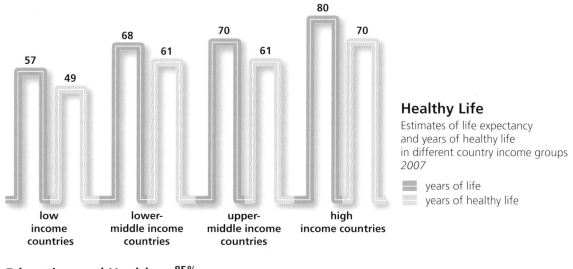

57

49

68

61

70

61

80

70

low
income
countries

lower-
middle income
countries

upper-
middle income
countries

high
income countries

Healthy Life

Estimates of life expectancy
and years of healthy life
in different country income groups
2007

▦ years of life
▦ years of healthy life

Education and Health

Relationship between
percentage of infants
immunized against measles
and educational attainment
of mother
latest available 2000–07
countries where greatest
difference

▦ lowest educational
attainment
▦ highest educational
attainment

85%

36%

71%

32%

63%

30%

71%

30%

54%

18%

48%

24%

67%

16%

Madagascar Paraguay Ethiopia Zimbabwe Chad Somalia Nigeria

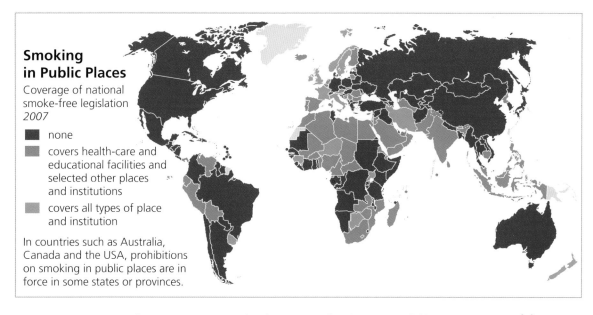

Smoking
in Public Places

Coverage of national
smoke-free legislation
2007

■ none
■ covers health-care and
educational facilities and
selected other places
and institutions
■ covers all types of place
and institution

In countries such as Australia,
Canada and the USA, prohibitions
on smoking in public places are in
force in some states or provinces.

Part 2

Judicial Violations & Legal Restrictions

The state occupies a difficult and often contradictory place within the field of human rights. On the one hand, the state is entrusted with the responsibility and legal duty of upholding, protecting, and promoting individuals' human rights. On the other hand, the state is the single greatest violator of human rights. This paradox raises complex problems and challenges for human rights defenders everywhere.

Not all states abuse human rights to the same degree; some are manifestly far worse than others. One important factor in determining the likelihood of states violating rather than protecting human rights is the secure establishment of the rule of law. States based upon a fundamental respect for the rule of law that enshrines international human rights principles are typically less guilty of directly violating human rights. However, many states and many state officials continue to ignore their own human rights commitments. Arguably the most prominent example of this is to be found in the re-emergence of state torture as a means for pursuing state policies or objectives. In recent years, the so-called "war on terror" has sparked the spectacle of several established democratic governments resorting to this most egregious human rights violation in the pursuit of suspected terrorists.

States which have resorted to torture have severely undermined their human rights credentials as a consequence. Other examples of states exceeding the rule of law are to be found in widespread forms of arbitrary detention and police brutality, both of which have been resorted to as a means to restrict many people's human rights. Another state violation of human rights consists of the continuing practice of capital punishment. While capital punishment may fall within the rule of law in those countries which retain the death penalty, the taking of life by the state is considered by many as a fundamental human rights violation.

CHINA: A woman shows a photograph or her son, held under sentence of death for over a decade on the basis of a confession made under torture.

Torture

Torture is expressly forbidden in all circumstances, without exception, under the terms of international human rights law. Despite the ratification by over 145 states of the Convention Against Torture, it remains widespread.

Torture is most likely to occur in places of detention or incarceration. Typically, torturers are agents of the state, while their victims are targeted on the basis that they pose some real or perceived threat to public order or national security. Torture is also deployed in otherwise far more mundane criminal investigations, typically as a means to extract confessions from the accused. Very few state officials are ever prosecuted for perpetrating acts of torture and very few states admit that their officials resort to torture.

The legal prohibition of torture belies long-standing issues over what precisely constitutes torture. Some argue that it may be morally legitimate in circumstances where the act of torturing a "guilty" individual will predictably avert much greater levels of human suffering being inflicted upon innocent human beings. The USA's so-called "war on terror" has had the effect of significantly raising the profile of torture within liberal-democratic countries. It has also reminded us that, despite being a flagrant human rights abuse, support for, and the practice of, torture are not restricted to overtly authoritarian countries.

The Szczytno Szymany airfield in Poland was used by the CIA for the extraordinary rendition of suspected terrorists during the US "war on terror". It is one of a number of so-called "black sites" implicated in the possible torture of detainees.

What the law says...

For the Purposes of this Convention, torture means any act by which severe pain or suffering, whether physical or mental, is intentionally inflicted on a person for such purposes as obtaining from him or a third person information, or a confession, punishing him for an act he or a third person has committed or is suspected of having committed, or intimidating or coercing him or a third person, for any reason based on intimidation or discrimination of any kind where such pain or suffering is inflicted by or at the instigation of or with the consent or acquiescence of a public official or other person acting in an official capacity.

UN Convention against Torture and Other Cruel, Inhuman or Degrading Treatment, 1984, Article 1

Torturers
2007–08

- torture cases documented
- foreign citizens returned from these countries to ones where they face the likelihood of torture
- no data

CANADA

USA

BRAZIL Brazil has one of the largest per capita prison populations in the world. The conditions in prisons and detention centres are appalling. Torturing those in pre-trial detention is reportedly endemic.

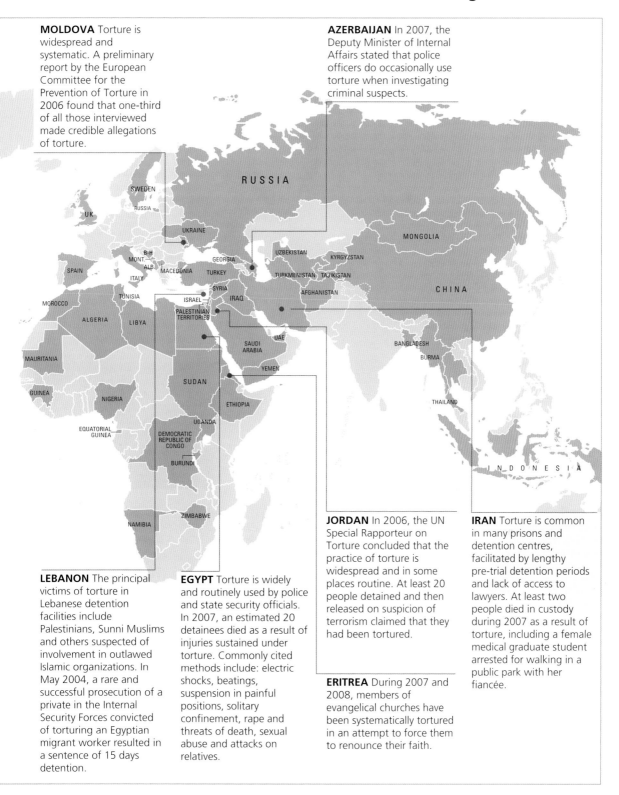

MOLDOVA Torture is widespread and systematic. A preliminary report by the European Committee for the Prevention of Torture in 2006 found that one-third of all those interviewed made credible allegations of torture.

AZERBAIJAN In 2007, the Deputy Minister of Internal Affairs stated that police officers do occasionally use torture when investigating criminal suspects.

JORDAN In 2006, the UN Special Rapporteur on Torture concluded that the practice of torture is widespread and in some places routine. At least 20 people detained and then released on suspicion of terrorism claimed that they had been tortured.

IRAN Torture is common in many prisons and detention centres, facilitated by lengthy pre-trial detention periods and lack of access to lawyers. At least two people died in custody during 2007 as a result of torture, including a female medical graduate student arrested for walking in a public park with her fiancée.

LEBANON The principal victims of torture in Lebanese detention facilities include Palestinians, Sunni Muslims and others suspected of involvement in outlawed Islamic organizations. In May 2004, a rare and successful prosecution of a private in the Internal Security Forces convicted of torturing an Egyptian migrant worker resulted in a sentence of 15 days detention.

EGYPT Torture is widely and routinely used by police and state security officials. In 2007, an estimated 20 detainees died as a result of injuries sustained under torture. Commonly cited methods include: electric shocks, beatings, suspension in painful positions, solitary confinement, rape and threats of death, sexual abuse and attacks on relatives.

ERITREA During 2007 and 2008, members of evangelical churches have been systematically tortured in an attempt to force them to renounce their faith.

Arbitrary Detention

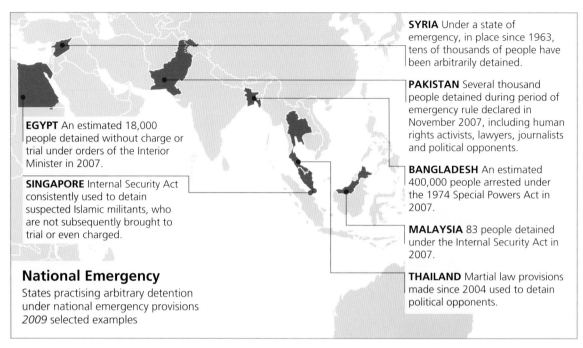

SYRIA Under a state of emergency, in place since 1963, tens of thousands of people have been arbitrarily detained.

PAKISTAN Several thousand people detained during period of emergency rule declared in November 2007, including human rights activists, lawyers, journalists and political opponents.

EGYPT An estimated 18,000 people detained without charge or trial under orders of the Interior Minister in 2007.

SINGAPORE Internal Security Act consistently used to detain suspected Islamic militants, who are not subsequently brought to trial or even charged.

BANGLADESH An estimated 400,000 people arrested under the 1974 Special Powers Act in 2007.

MALAYSIA 83 people detained under the Internal Security Act in 2007.

THAILAND Martial law provisions made since 2004 used to detain political opponents.

National Emergency

States practising arbitrary detention under national emergency provisions *2009* selected examples

---

One of the principal powers of any state is the capacity to detain and imprison people, but some use unfair and arbitrary detention as a means of political control.

All functioning states enforce the law and, where necessary, lawfully detain, put on trial and sentence those found guilty of infringing criminal laws, but in many countries, safeguards exist to ensure that these powers are exercised in accordance with established principles of legal justice.

The International Covenant on Civil and Political Rights has been ratified by over 160 states, but some continue to use unfair and arbitrary detention as a mechanism of control, abusing the human rights of their citizens. Unfair and arbitrary detention is often practised under the terms of state or national emergency provisions. Other instances of this human rights abuse are pursued without any resort to the semblance of international legality.

Of those people arbitrarily detained, many have attracted the attention of the state purely as a consequence of pursuing peaceful political activities. Some of these have been tried and convicted and may be identified as political prisoners. Various legal mechanisms, such as state-of-emergency provisions, allegations of treason, public-order legislation and sedition are used to provide a veneer of legal legitimacy to political oppression.

...an estimated **500,000 people in China** are subjected to **punitive detention** without charge or trial...

Camp Delta in Guantánamo Bay has galvanized opposition to the detention by the USA of people it suspects of practising terrorism. In 2009, President Obama promised to close it down.

What the law says...

Everyone has the right to liberty and security of person. No one shall be subjected to arbitrary arrest or detention. No one shall be deprived of his liberty except on such grounds and in accordance with such procedure as are established by law.

International Covenant on Civil and Political Rights, 1966, Article 9

Judicial Violations & Legal Restrictions

GREECE Greek authorities accused of arbitrarily detaining migrants and asylum seekers, against EU regulations

GAMBIA Journalists and political opponents subject to arbitrary detention.

EQUATORIAL GUINEA Arbitrary detention persistently used as a form of political oppression over many years.

BURUNDI 112 arbitrary arrests documented in January 2007. Several hundred more estimated.

ANGOLA The regime of President Dos Santos has been accused of numerous arbitrary arrests and detentions of political opponents.

IRAQ 60,000 prisoners were being detained without charge by the Multinational Force and the Iraqi security forces in November 2007.

ISRAEL and PALESTINIAN TERRITORIES
Israel was holding over 9,000 Palestinian adults and children without charge or trial in 2007. Many had been detained for several years.

Hamas militias in Gaza detained 1,500 people, mostly members of the rival Fatah movement during 2007.

SRI LANKA Authorities detained over 1,000 Tamils as a response to suicide bombings in Colombo during late 2007.

PHILIPPINES Arbitrary detention of political activists and politicians takes place.

Arbitrary Detention

States practising
arbitrary detention
2009 selected examples

Chained prisoners, among them political detainees, at a forced labour camp in Kachin, Burma. They are constructing army facilities in Myitkyina, the state capital.

Political Prisoners

States holding
political prisoners
2009 selected examples

SYRIA An estimated 4,000 political prisoners were held in 2008, mostly comprising members of the Muslim Brotherhood and the Communist Party. 1,500 were imprisoned in 2007 alone.

ERITREA Several hundred political opponents were imprisoned between 2001 and 2008, including 11 former government ministers and liberation veterans being held in secret detention for calling for democratic reforms.

CUBA An estimated 220 political prisoners who oppose the Cuban regime's continued restrictions upon democratic participation were being held in 2008.

ETHIOPIA Several hundred members of an opposition party were detained in 2005 and were still being detained without trial in 2008.

BURMA An estimated 2,100 political prisoners were being held in 2008, over 1,000 of whom were participants in the 2007–08 so-called "Saffron" protests.

CHINA An estimated 16,460 political prisoners were being held in 2008, from a wide range of political and ethnic groups.

Capital Punishment

The death penalty raises complex and very serious human rights issues. Punishment by death is a long-established feature of many religious traditions, and also unites otherwise quite different societies, such as the USA and China.

Opponents of the death penalty typically base their arguments on Articles 3 and 5 of the Universal Declaration of Human Rights (UDHR). Article 3 is clearly incompatible with judicial or extra-judicial killing, whereas article 5 applies more specifically to the conditions in which the convicted are held up until their execution and the manner in which the sentence is carried out. In the USA, for example, condemned people may be held on death row for many years, if not decades, prior to their execution. This is considered by many to contribute to the cruel, inhumane and degrading nature of the punishment.

In addition to the UDHR, the Second Optional Protocol to the International Covenant on Civil and Political Rights characterizes the death penalty as a fundamental violation of human rights and represents the most concerted international attempt to abolish it. Although only 71 UN member-states were party to it by 2009, the number of signatories is steadily increasing. Nearly 70 countries that have not formally abolished the death penalty do not, in practice, make use of it.

International Instruments against Death Penalty

UN unanimously adopts the Universal Declaration of Human Rights.

1948

...**death sentences** in USA 1976–2007: **79%** were cases in which **homicide victims** were **white**...

Methods of Execution

Different countries and cultures use different methods. They include:

- beheading
- electrocution
- hanging
- lethal injection
- shooting
- stoning

What the law says...

Everyone has the right to life, liberty and security of person....No one shall be subjected to torture or to cruel, inhuman or degrading treatment or punishment.

Universal Declaration of Human Rights, 1948, articles 3 and 5

No one within the jurisdiction of a State Party to the present Protocol shall be executed.

Second Optional Protocol to the International Covenant on Civil and Political Rights, aiming at the abolition of the death penalty, 1989

Judicial Violations & Legal Restrictions

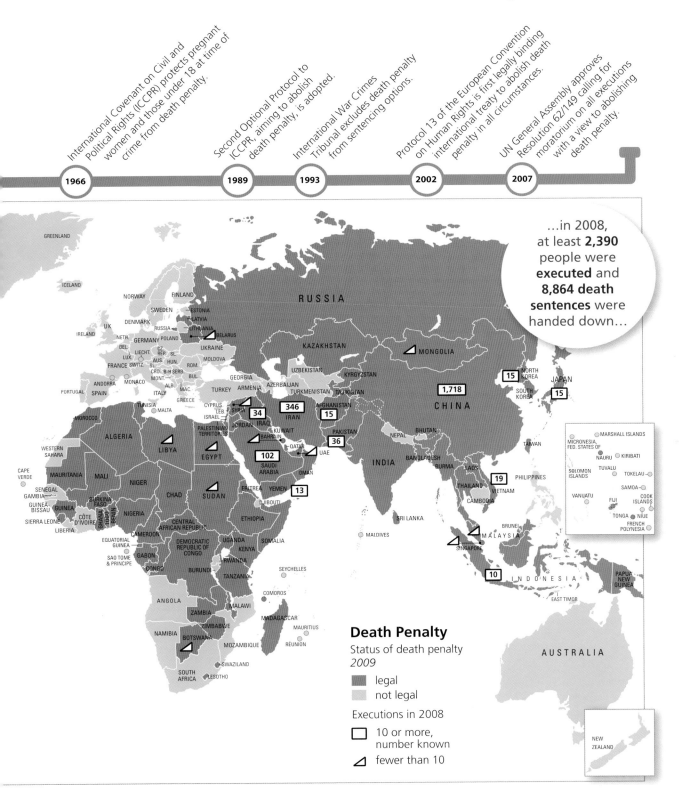

International Covenant on Civil and Political Rights (ICCPR) protects pregnant women and those under 18 at time of crime from death penalty.

1966

Second Optional Protocol to ICCPR, aiming to abolish death penalty, is adopted.

1989

International War Crimes Tribunal excludes death penalty from sentencing options.

1993

Protocol 13 of the European Convention on Human Rights is first legally binding international treaty to abolish death penalty in all circumstances.

2002

UN General Assembly approves Resolution 62/149 calling for moratorium on all executions with a view to abolishing death penalty.

2007

...in 2008, at least **2,390** people were **executed** and **8,864 death sentences** were handed down...

Death Penalty

Status of death penalty
2009

- legal
- not legal

Executions in 2008

- ☐ 10 or more, number known
- ◿ fewer than 10

Policing

Governments have a fundamental duty to protect the security of their citizens, but far too often police officers become violators, rather than protectors, of citizens' human rights.

Police forces play a crucial role in ensuring that law-abiding citizens are free from assaults upon their person and property. They also have a crucial role in enabling the exercise of fundamental human rights, such as those to peaceful assembly and protest.

Unfortunately, human rights supporters across the world have all too often encountered suspicion and even outright hostility from police officials. In many instances, this hostility has extended to include police officers violating human rights in numerous ways. These include the unlawful killing, torture and mistreatment of people taken into custody, the physical abuse and intimidation of people suspected of committing crimes, the killing of innocent protesters, and the use of unjustified and excessive force in policing public demonstrations.

Discriminatory Policing

Ethnic background of people stopped and searched by London police compared with ethnic distribution in city population
2000–07

▓ Asian
▓ African-Caribbean
░ white
▒ other/not known

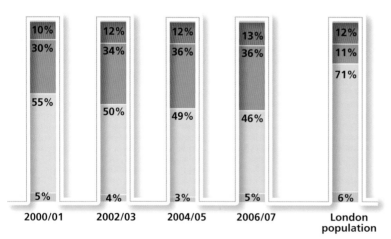

All citizens have a fundamental human right not to be discriminated against on the grounds of race or ethnicity. The statistics on the ethnic backgrounds of people stopped, searched and questioned indicate that a disproportionately high number of African-Caribbean people are targeted by police officers.

Police Violations of Human Rights

Selected examples

USA The UN Committee Against Torture has recognized that the use of the TASER, which administers an electric shock to render people incapable, can amount to cruel, inhuman, and degrading treatment or punishment. Between 2001 and 2006, over 150 people died in police custody after being shocked with TASERs.

USA A 2006 survey by the New Orleans organization Safe Streets/Strong Communities found that 72% of the predominantly African-American respondents who had been stopped by police reported being victimized – through verbal abuse, public strip searches, or physical abuse.

BAHAMAS Emmanuel McKenzie, an environmental activist, was harassed and ill-treated by the security forces in a joint army/police raid on a fundraising event in 2008. He was handcuffed, dragged off to a clearing and had a gun pointed at his head. Some of those attending the event were also beaten and ill-treated.

VENEZUELA Police are estimated to be responsible for 900 killings each year, and the Minister of Interior and Justice, Tariq El-Aissami, admitted in 2009 that 20% of all crimes in the country were committed by the police

UK In 2005, police officers shot dead a Brazilian, Jean Charles de Menezes, at point-blank range on a London underground train. De Menezes, who was entirely innocent, had been mistaken for a suspected terrorist bomber in an operation that was subsequently heavily criticized. No prosecutions have been brought against any police official.

ALBANIA Police are alleged to have tortured or ill-treated people, minors included, in over 140 incidents from 2002–05.

BANGLADESH In 2008, despite a lifting of the ban on political rallies, police used sticks and rifle butts to disperse a peaceful rally, injuring at least 30 demonstrators.

SYRIA In 2007, the Syrian government failed to acknowledge security-force involvement in the "disappearances" of an estimated 17,000 persons since the 1970s, the vast majority of whom remain unaccounted for and many of whom are believed to have been killed by Syrian forces or while in their custody.

CÔTE D'IVOIRE In 2008, riot police dispersed several hundred demonstrators who had blocked roads and burned tyres in Abidjan, to protest against the rising cost of staple foods. The police used tear gas grenades and live ammunition. Two people were killed and more than 10 people, including women traders, were wounded.

KENYA More than 1,000 people were killed as a result of politically motivated ethnic violence and associated police killings following disputed elections in 2007. The government failed to investigate allegations of torture and unlawful killings committed by the police, including the execution of this woman's brother and nine other men.

INDIA Srinagar, Kashmir In 2008, protests in Jammu and Kashmir erupted into violence on several occasions. Police used excessive force and shot dead more than 60 people.

Part 3

Freedom of Expression & Censorship

A vibrant civil society is generally considered to be essential for the protection of civil and political rights. Civil society offers a space which is free from undue state regulation and interference within which individuals and groups may express themselves, debate with others, challenge prevailing orthodoxies, freely associate with like-minded individuals, and form groups and communities for the protection and promotion of specific interests and concerns.

The protection and promotion of everybody's human rights does require placing some restrictions on some aspects of civil society. For example, many argue that freedom of expression should not extend to include so-called "hate speech" or forms of expression or association which seek to incite violence and hatred against others. The precise point at which legitimate forms of expression and association are to be distinguished from their illegitimate, human-rights-threatening counterparts remains a matter of intense debate in many countries.

Beyond the realm of legitimate restrictions, many peoples across the world are confronted by wholesale and thoroughly illegitimate state interference in respect of what they would seek to say, or with whom they would wish to associate. Many states impose severe restrictions on people's ability to publicly criticize the state, the government, the nation, the prevailing religion or state ideology, and many other such public bodies, symbols and institutions. Not surprisingly, these measures have impacted particularly heavily upon journalists and independent media outlets.

In recent years, the development of the internet has created a new space for free expression and association, and with it a new challenge to state censorship. Thus, a significant number of states have created forms of surveillance and censorship of the internet and, in so doing, have sought to frustrate the development of this cyber civil society.

TAIWAN: People protest against the People's Republic of China.

Freedom of Speech

The expression of opinions and views is widely considered a fundamental attribute of individual freedom.

The right to freedom of expression and speech is enshrined in Article 19 of the International Covenant on Civil and Political Rights, although both the text of the covenant and widely held views recognize the need to limit this right under certain circumstances. Forms of expression and speech likely to result in significant infringements of the fundamental rights of others – such as "hate speech" or overtly defamatory utterances – are liable to restriction, which, within international law, may also be applied for the protection of national security, public order or public health and morals.

This restriction is open to abuse. Numerous states have systematically utilized this mechanism in an attempt to curtail the freedom of speech and expression of those who challenge and seek to expose human rights abuses and forms of political oppression.

Not surprisingly, the group of people whose right to freedom of expression and speech has been most likely to be violated and restricted are journalists. These violations take many forms, from conventional censorship and prohibition to imprisonment and even death. In recent years, anti-state allegations such as subversion, divulging state secrets, and acting against national interests have been the most common charges used to imprison journalists throughout the world. The rise of the internet is reflected in the fact that 45 percent of all media workers jailed worldwide are bloggers, web-based reporters, or online editors.

Abuse of Journalists in 2008

- 60 killed
- 929 physically attacked or threatened
- 29 kidnapped
- 673 arrested

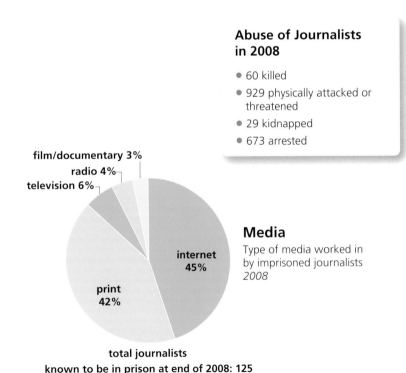

film/documentary 3%
radio 4%
television 6%
internet 45%
print 42%

Media
Type of media worked in by imprisoned journalists
2008

**total journalists
known to be in prison at end of 2008: 125**

Media Freedom under Threat
Reporters without Borders index of press freedom
2009

- 76.0 or worse
- 51.0 – 75.9
- 26.0 – 50.9
- better than 26.0
- no data

The index score is based on reports of violations of press freedom.

Freedom of Expression & Censorship

...**60 journalists** were **killed** worldwide in **2008**...

AFGHANISTAN Parwiz Kambakhsh, a 23-year-old journalist, was imprisoned in 2007, accused of distributing anti-Islamic literature in Mazar-i-Sharif. A three-judge panel handed down a death penalty in closed session in 2008, but although the appellate court upheld the blasphemy sentence, it reduced the death sentence to a 20-year prison term.

CHINA This increasingly powerful country is the world's worst jailer of journalists, a dishonour it has held for 10 consecutive years. At the end of 2008, 28 journalists were held in its prisons.

RUSSIA Anna Politkovskaya, murdered in Moscow in 2006, was one of the few Russian journalists reporting on events in Chechnya. Her article on torture there had been due to appear in the *Novaya Gazeta*. Her killer has yet to be identified. In 2009, Natalia Estemirova, who campaigned for human rights in Chechnya, was also murdered.

IRAQ In 2008, 14 journalists were killed.

Communications Censorship

The capacity to seek, receive and impart information is central to the exercise of individual liberty, and is an essential attribute of a genuinely open society.

State censorship has imposed various forms of direct constraint upon what may be made available in the public domain. The protection of national security, state secrets, or the "spirit" of the nation are routinely cited as reasons to restrict the flow of information and opinion, and all states practise censorship to a greater or lesser degree.

The internet promised to be particularly valuable to people in countries where extensive censorship violated their human right to freely communicate, but the more repressive states have risen to the challenge it presents to their ability to censor and control the flow of information. So, far from being a new, genuinely free market of ideas and communication, the internet is now subject to increasingly sophisticated forms of censorship and surveillance.

Alongside the more traditional forms of censorship, such as the imprisonment, harassment and intimidation of journalists and bloggers, many states have developed methods for regulating and blocking citizens' access to those parts of the internet deemed unacceptable. This amounts to a violation of individual human rights, tends to stifle the development of civil society, and represents another tool in the armoury of political oppression.

Internet Censorship
Assessment made by OpenNet Initiative of level of filtering on political grounds
2009

- pervasive
- substantial
- selective
- suspected
- no evidence
- no data

● countries identified as "enemies of the internet" by Reporters Without Borders for their censorship of news and repression of internet users

CUBA
●

VENEZUELA

...**1,740 websites** were reported **blocked, shut down** or **suspended** worldwide in 2008...

Media Outlets Closed
Number recorded by Reporters Without Frontiers
2008

- Africa: 41
- Asia/Pacific: 70
- Americas: 72
- Europe and Central Asia: 79
- North Africa and Middle-East: 91

Freedom of Expression & Censorship

SWITZERLAND While other European countries routinely block access to sites carrying child pornography or overtly racist material, the Swiss authorities take a more widespread approach. In 2002, a Swiss magistrate ordered several Swiss internet providers to block access to selected US sites on the grounds that these had been consistently critical of Swiss courts.

TURKEY In 2007, it took the Turkish parliament less than an hour to debate and enact legislation intended to provide more effective regulation of access to the internet. In two years the number of sites blocked under this legislation rose to 2,600. Turkey also systematically blocks access to YouTube.

IRAN All internet communications must pass through a single portal: the Telecommunications Company of Iran. A committee of government officials and members of the judiciary and intelligence services meets regularly to determine which sites are to be blocked or scrutinized by the Ministry of Telecommunications.

SOUTH KOREA With over 89% of households having access, South Korea is the most internet-connected country in the world. The authorities monitor internet communications, and expressions of support or praise for the government of North Korea are systematically blocked and censored.

CHINA The government plan to bundle internet filtering software in all computers was met with widespread protest from among China's 300 million online community, and was postponed in June 2009. Existing methods of internet censorship, such as blocking access to particular sites, and self-censorship by internet giants such as Google, continue unabated. During ethnic riots in Xinjiang in 2009, which resulted in at least 140 deaths, the internet in the region was shut down, and Twitter was blocked throughout the country.

RUSSIA

RUSSIA
BELARUS
UKRAINE
MOLDOVA
KAZAKHSTAN
UZBEKISTAN
AZERBAIJAN
KYRGYZSTAN
TURKMEN.
TAJIKISTAN
AFGHAN.
TUNISIA
ISRAEL
SYRIA
IRAQ
JORDAN
IRAN
PAKISTAN
ALGERIA
LIBYA
EGYPT
SAUDI ARABIA
UAE
OMAN
NEPAL
INDIA
NORTH KOREA
CHINA
BURMA
VIETNAM
THAILAND
MALAYSIA
SUDAN
YEMEN
ETHIOPIA
ZIMBABWE

TUNISIA In July 2009, a retired professor, Dr Khedija Arfaoui, was condemned to eight months in prison for disrupting public order by suggesting on Facebook that five children had been abducted from a school in Tunis. There are widespread fears that children are being abducted and trafficked and, despite a recent denial by a government minister, these fears persist.

SAUDI ARABIA The Saud regime has been condemned as the worst internet censor among the Arab countries. Sites carrying political, religious or "immoral" material are targeted, as are those belonging to opposition or human rights groups.

UZBEKISTAN While its constitution proclaims freedom of expression and prohibits state censorship, Uzbekistan practises extensive internet monitoring and censorship, which has increased significantly since the violent protests in Tashkent and the province of Andijan in 2004. Methods deployed include software penetration, severe restrictions on ISPs and encouraging media self-censorship.

BURMA A state licence is required for possessing and using a modem, with a 15-year prison sentence the penalty for breaking the law. Fourteen journalists and two bloggers were in prison in 2009. A comedian, Zarganar, received a 35-year prison sentence for posting articles on the internet criticizing the authorities' management of humanitarian aid following Cyclone Nargis.

Assembly & Association

Meeting with and relating to others is an essential feature of citizenship, yet restrictions on the right to assemble remain a central tool by which notional "democracies" and overtly authoritarian regimes thwart and distort the will of the people.

Freedom of assembly and of association are recognized by the International Convenant on Civil and Political Rights as two separate rights, but both continue to be systematically violated around the globe, despite being ratified by all but 29 states. Many states restrict peaceful assembly in the name of national security or public order – often simply a spurious justification for the repression of legitimate political action. Others restrict almost all forms of assembly, especially around the time of elections.

The right to freedom of association emerges out of, and tends to focus on, attempts to protect the conditions of workers. Article 22 enshrines the right of workers to form or join trade unions, and provides for the pursuit of industrial action. The lack of a viable economic alternative to capitalism, and the apparent erosion of distinct and integral "working-class" identities in many industrialized and post-industrialized societies, have contributed to the demise of the global trade union movement's influence and membership. Other factors, such as the lobbying power of big business, the bargaining power of transnational corporations and a general prioritization of economic interests over other concerns have simultaneously contributed to ongoing violations of article 22.

What the law says...

Everyone shall have the right to freedom of association with others, including the right to form and join trade unions for the protection of his interests.

International Convenant on Civil and Political Rights, 1966, Article 22

What the law says...

The right of peaceful assembly shall be recognized. No restrictions may be placed on the exercise of this right other than those imposed in conformity with the law and which are necessary in a democratic society in the interests of national security or public safety, public order, the protection of public health or morals or the protection of the rights and freedoms of others.

International Convenant on Civil and Political Rights, 1966, Article 21

Iranians take to the streets to protest the outcome of the 2009 Presidential elections, which resulted in an unexpectedly large majority for Ahmedinajad. The protests were deemed to be illegal and resulted in bloody clashes with the police and security forces.

Freedom of Association under Threat

Freedom House index of freedom to associate
2007

- ■ 0 – 3 *heavy restrictions*
- ■ 4 – 6
- ■ 7 – 9
- □ 10 – 12 *light restrictions*
- ▨ no data

CANADA

BAHAMAS
CUBA
MEXICO
DOMINICAN REP.
JAMAICA
HAITI
BELIZE
GUATEMALA HONDURAS ST KITTS & NEVIS ANTIGUA & BARBUDA
EL SALVADOR NICARAGUA DOMINICA
GRENADA ST VINCENT & GRENADINES
COSTA RICA BARBADOS
PANAMA VENEZUELA TRINIDAD & TOBAGO
GUYANA
COLOMBIA SURINAME
ECUADOR
PERU
BRAZIL
BOLIVIA
CHILE PARAGUAY
ARGENTINA
URUGUAY

USA The National Labor Relations Act (NLRA) guarantees the right to freedom of association, to bargain collectively, and for private-sector employees to join trade unions. But as well as excluding public-sector workers, it also excludes many in the private sector, including agricultural and domestic workers, supervisors, and independent contractors. In 2002, around 25 million private workers, and 6.9 million federal, state and local government employees, had no right under any law to negotiate wages, hours or employment terms. Since then, even more workers have been denied coverage.

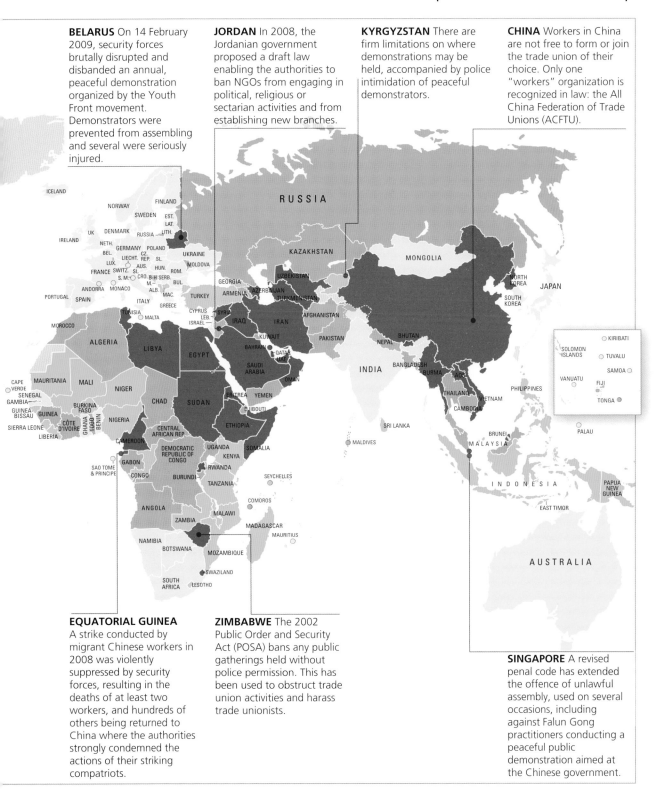

BELARUS On 14 February 2009, security forces brutally disrupted and disbanded an annual, peaceful demonstration organized by the Youth Front movement. Demonstrators were prevented from assembling and several were seriously injured.

JORDAN In 2008, the Jordanian government proposed a draft law enabling the authorities to ban NGOs from engaging in political, religious or sectarian activities and from establishing new branches.

KYRGYZSTAN There are firm limitations on where demonstrations may be held, accompanied by police intimidation of peaceful demonstrators.

CHINA Workers in China are not free to form or join the trade union of their choice. Only one "workers" organization is recognized in law: the All China Federation of Trade Unions (ACFTU).

EQUATORIAL GUINEA A strike conducted by migrant Chinese workers in 2008 was violently suppressed by security forces, resulting in the deaths of at least two workers, and hundreds of others being returned to China where the authorities strongly condemned the actions of their striking compatriots.

ZIMBABWE The 2002 Public Order and Security Act (POSA) bans any public gatherings held without police permission. This has been used to obstruct trade union activities and harass trade unionists.

SINGAPORE A revised penal code has extended the offence of unlawful assembly, used on several occasions, including against Falun Gong practitioners conducting a peaceful public demonstration aimed at the Chinese government.

Part 4

Conflict & Migration

Some of the most visible human rights violations result from conflict and migration, which have characterized human societies since time immemorial. Human beings are, in many respects, their own worst enemy.

The modern human rights movement emerged out of the Second World War and is a response, in particular, to the atrocities and horror of the Holocaust. A principal aim of human rights conventions is the prevention of conflict and the causes of forced and mass migration. Despite the best intentions of many human rights defenders, genocide did not end with the Holocaust and there have been several million victims of genocide in various parts of the globe since the end of the Second World War. Likewise, ongoing wars and forms of armed conflict continue to impose heavy costs on the human rights of populations exposed to them, including loss of life and whole populations fleeing the fighting in search of refuge and asylum.

The United Nations has actively sought to prevent the escalation of armed conflict in many parts of the world through the deployment of blue-helmeted UN Peacekeepers. However, all such missions have a mandate to keep an already established "peace" or cessation of hostilities. UN Peacekeepers are characteristically deployed once the worst of the fighting is over.

Many people's dream of achieving world peace is undermined by the existence and scale of the global arms trade. Arms production and exports make sizeable contributions to the economies of many of the leading members of the international community, including countries who consistently affirm their commitment to peace and stability.

There can be no doubt that the effects of continuing conflict and instability are devastating the human rights of countless millions of people. A genuine commitment to the prevention of such abuses will require far-reaching actions and policies by those both directly and indirectly involved in the perpetuation of human misery.

CHAD: A young soldier in the Justice and Equality Movement militia prepares to fight the Janjaweed.

Genocide

The drafting of the Universal Declaration of Human Rights was in part a reaction to the horrors of the Holocaust. The urge to prevent genocide is thus one of the central elements of the modern human rights movement.

Which atrocities may legitimately be considered as "genocide" is frequently a matter of dispute. Defining an ongoing conflict as genocidal places a legal obligation on the UN to take action and is thus a heavily politicized issue. Defining a prior conflict as genocidal has implications for relations between states and the claims of victims' descendants to reparation.

Holocaust denial is illegal in 10 European states, including Austria, France, Germany and Poland. By contrast, in Turkey it is illegal to claim that the death of 1.5 million Armenians in 1914–18 was an act of genocide.

What the law says...

Genocide refers to any of the following acts committed with intent to destroy, in whole or in part, a national, ethnic, racial or religious group, including: (a) killing members of the group, (b) causing serious bodily or mental harm to members of the group, (c) deliberately inflicting on the group conditions of life calculated to bring about its physical destruction in whole or in part, (d) imposing measures intended to prevent births within the group, (e) forcibly transferring children of the group to another group.

UN Convention on the Prevention and Punishment of the Crime of Genocide, 1948, Article 2

20th-century Genocides

1914 –18 1.5m Armenians, victims of Ottoman Turkey

1932 –33 3m Ukrainians, victims of Stalin's Soviet Union

1937 –38 300,000 Chinese in Nanjing, victims of Japanese Imperial Army

1941 –45 6m Jews, victims of Nazi Germany

650,000 Serbs, Jews and Roma in the Balkans, victims of the Croatian Ustache

1962 –96 200,000 Mayan Indians, victims of Guatemalan government forces

1971 3m Bangladeshis, victims of Pakistan forces in what was then East Pakistan

1972 100,000 Hutus, victims of the Tutsi-dominated Burundi regime

1975 –79 3m Cambodians, victims of Pol Pot's Khmer Rouge regime

1975 –90s 300,000 East Timorese, victims of political repression

1986 –89 200,000 Kurds, victims of Saddam Hussein's campaign against Kurds in Iraq

1993 50,000 Tutsis, victims of Hutu-dominated Burundi regime

1994 800,000 mostly Tutsis, victims of Hutu massacres in Rwanda

1995 8,000 Bosnian Muslims, killed in Srebrenica by Serb forces

Areas of Concern

Countries experiencing systematic mass killing and atrocities that could develop into genocide
2009

DEMOCRATIC REPUBLIC OF THE CONGO Decades of conflict between war-lord militia has resulted in the death of at least 2.5 million civilians, many of them deliberately targeted by different ethnic factions. Over 1.5 million displaced people are living in camps, as are nearly 370,000 refugees who have fled conflict in neighbouring countries.

...in the 20th century
72.5 million deaths
resulted from
genocides...

Conflict & Migration

ISRAEL and PALESTINIAN TERRITORIES Thousands of civilians have died in the decades-long conflict between Palestinian militia groups and the Israeli army, either deliberately or as "collateral damage" in the targeting of military opponents.

IRAQ The sectarian violence that erupted following the fall of Saddam Hussein's regime in 2003 has resulted in the death of nearly 100,000 civilians, the majority of them deliberately targeted by opposing religious factions.

AFGHANISTAN Civilians have been dying as the result of conflict in the country for decades, but since 2001 thousands have been killed by Taliban action, or as the result of military action by NATO forces.

BURMA The military junta is ruthless in its oppression of ethnic minority groups, political opponents and Buddhist monks. The refusal of the government to allow international aid agencies to enter the country following Cyclone Nargis in 2008 led to the unnecessary deaths of untold thousands of civilians.

CHAD Since 2005, Sudan-backed militias have killed thousands of Zaghawas and Fur.

SOMALIA The effective disintegration of the state has left civilians unprotected against the atrocities inflicted on them by armed groups and criminal gangs.

SUDAN Since 2004, government-backed Arab militia, the Janjaweed, have waged war on ethnic Africans in the region of Darfur, killing at least 400,000 and driving hundreds of thousands more from their homes to live in makeshift shelters or refugee camps. Although the USA has declared this to be a campaign of genocide, the UN has declined to classify it as such on the basis of a 2005 report that concluded that genocidal intent was lacking.

SRI LANKA The civil war between Tamil Tiger rebels and the Sri Lankan government army ended in 2009 with the defeat of the rebels. During the conflict, atrocities were committed against civilians by both sides. Communities were devastated – their inhabitants killed or driven out, the buildings destroyed and the fields strewn with unexploded ordnance. Thousands of people simply disappeared.

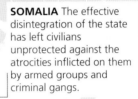

War & Armed Conflict

War and armed conflict have a devastating impact on human rights, not only the rights to life and physical security, but numerous other rights that are undermined by chaos and destruction.

Yet, armed intervention raises difficult questions for supporters of human rights. There is no specific human right to be free from the effects of warfare and armed conflict. Indeed, the UN Charter establishes the right of member states to resort to war as a means for securing and defending their sovereign territory. Article 28 of the Universal Declaration of Human Rights establishes a right to a "social and international order in which the rights and freedoms set forth in the Declaration can be fully realized". Some have interpreted this as entailing the deployment of military forces in order to combat so-called rogue states and prevent systematic violations of human rights.

In the context of human rights, war and armed conflict are double-edged in that their effects are devastating for people caught up in them, but the deployment of military forces remains one of the tools of last resort for restricting systematic threats to human rights.

Not all armed conflicts are between sovereign states. Almost half are being fought between warlords and militias and do not involve government forces.

Legal Status of Gulf Wars

1990
2 Aug – Iraq invades Kuwait. UN Security Council Resolution 660 calls for full withdrawal.
6 Aug – UNSC Resolution 661 imposes economic sanctions on Iraq.
29 Nov – UNSC Resolution 678 authorizes states cooperating with Kuwait to use "all necessary means" to uphold UNSC Resolution 660.

1991
16 Jan to 3 Mar – The Gulf War. Coalition forces conduct aerial bombardment of Iraq, followed by ground attack, driving Iraqi forces out of Kuwait. Iraq accepts the terms of a ceasefire.

1992–2003
Following attacks by Iraqi air force on Kurds and Shi'a, USA and UK establish protective "no-fly zones". Although these are not specifically sanctioned by UNSC, the USA and UK argue they are consistent with UNSC Resolution 688, 5 April 1991.

1998
UNSC asserts that Council members cannot act unilaterally to enforce resolutions.

2002
12 Sept – President George W. Bush tells UN General Assembly that USA may be justified in taking pre-emptive military action against Iraq.
17 Sept – Bush outlines the "Bush Doctrine", which asserts that USA is willing to act unilaterally in pre-emptive self-defence.
8 Nov – UNSC unanimously passes Resolution 1441, which calls for the disarming of any Iraqi weapons of mass destruction. UNSC members disagree on whether it provides sufficient justification for an invasion of Iraq.

2003
20 March – US missile attacks on Baghdad mark the beginning of armed hostilities.
9 April – US forces take Baghdad.
May – UNSC backs US-led administration in Iraq.

2003 –05
Iraq Survey Group seeks and fails to find evidence of Weapons of Mass Destruction.

War at Home

Number of armed conflicts involving government forces fought within a country or its territorial waters *1946–2005*

- 13
- 7 – 9
- 4 – 6
- 1 – 3
- 0
- no data

country has been involved in at least 7 conflicts on home soil or overseas *1946–2005*

...more than **2 million died** in the **Vietnam War** 1955–75...

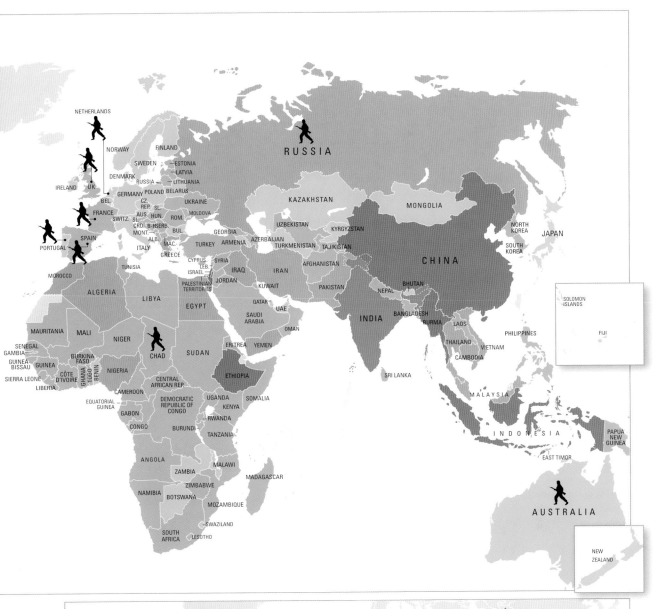

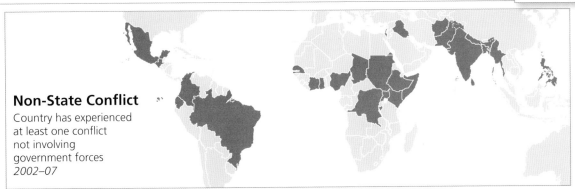

Non-State Conflict
Country has experienced
at least one conflict
not involving
government forces
2002–07

Arms Trade

Access to arms and weaponry continues to have a devastating effect on the human rights of people exposed to the bloody conflicts that blight the world.

While it is true that "guns don't kill people – people kill people", the global arms industry and the largely unregulated export of arms provide the means by which conflict is fuelled and maintained. The arms trade impacts on human rights when it helps politically oppressive regimes to remain in power, and encourages governments of poor countries to spend money on weapons rather than on education and healthcare.

Ineffective regulation of the arms trade means there can be no guarantee that, once acquired by governments, arms will be used for purely defensive purposes, or that they will not fall into the "wrong" hands. It is no coincidence that those with the most influence in the United Nations by virtue of their permanent seat on the Security Council – France, Russia, UK and the USA – are among those who gain the most from arms exports. In general, the most economically developed nations of the world constitute the main exporters of arms, while those of the developing world are the largest importers.

One form of arms, in particular, has exerted a terrible toll: landmines. Comparatively cheap to purchase, they are an entirely indiscriminate weapon and continue to kill and maim long after hostilities have ceased.

Between 15,000 and 20,000 people each year are killed or injured by landmines and unexploded ordnance, the majority from countries no longer in conflict. The impact of the presence of landmines reaches beyond the devastating physical damage they cause individuals. They can arrest the economic and social development of whole communities.

Persistent Killers

Countries that have experienced casualties from landmines and/or explosive remnants of war
2007

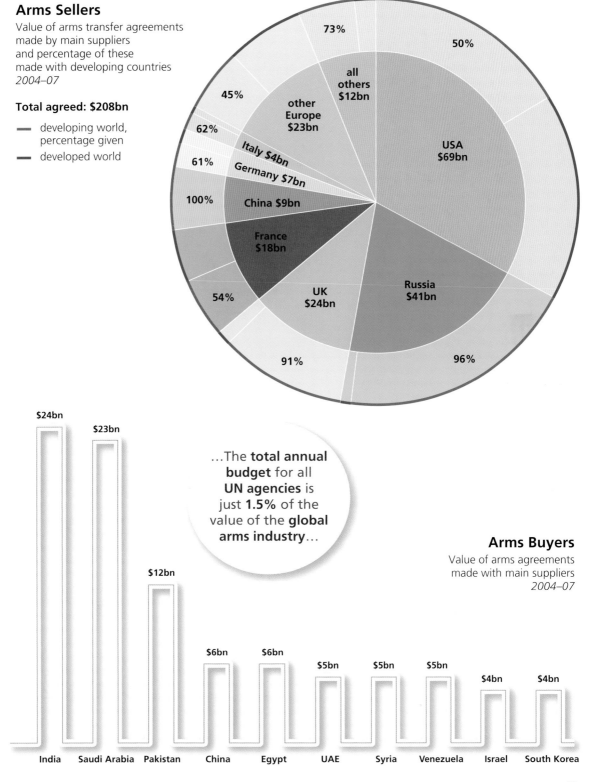

Arms Sellers

Value of arms transfer agreements
made by main suppliers
and percentage of these
made with developing countries
2004–07

Total agreed: $208bn

— developing world,
  percentage given
— developed world

73%

50%

all
others
$12bn

other
Europe
$23bn

45%

62%

Italy $4bn

61%

Germany $7bn

100%

China $9bn

France
$18bn

USA
$69bn

Russia
$41bn

UK
$24bn

54%

91%

96%

…The **total annual budget** for all **UN agencies** is just **1.5%** of the value of the **global arms industry**…

Arms Buyers

Value of arms agreements
made with main suppliers
2004–07

$24bn

$23bn

$12bn

$6bn

$6bn

$5bn

$5bn

$5bn

$4bn

$4bn

India   Saudi Arabia   Pakistan   China   Egypt   UAE   Syria   Venezuela   Israel   South Korea

Terrorism

Terrorism exists throughout the world today and is fundamentally incompatible with respect for human rights.

Despite this, the relationship between terrorism and human rights is complex and multi-faceted. Perpetrators of terrorist acts typically aim to gain maximum publicity and awareness of a particular cause by targeting specific victims.

Thousands of innocent civilians from around the globe have died in recent years as a consequence of terrorist atrocities, but the greatest attention has been paid to western victims, such as those who perished in the World Trade Center towers in New York, the bombing of a tourist area in Bali, and the suicide bombs on public transport in Madrid and London. Examples of so-called "Islamist terrorism", these acts were clearly designed to inflict maximum damage upon populations whose governments are considered to be pursuing hostile policies towards Islam. Defenders of these acts of terrorism justify their position by pointing to the violation of the human rights of Muslims in places such as Palestine, Afghanistan and Iraq. They accuse western powers of practising a form of state terrorism.

Both terrorism itself, and the response to it, constitute serious obstacles to the protection and promotion of human rights. While states have a fundamental duty to protect the lives and rights of their citizens, the response of some western governments to the terrorist threat has raised serious concerns for the human rights of those suspected of involvement in terrorism.

Acts of Terrorism
Selected events
2000–09

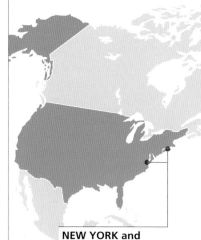

NEW YORK and WASHINGTON DC, USA, 2001 Al Qaida terrorists crashed three airliners into the World Trade Center and the Pentagon, killing 2,973 people of more than 50 nationalities.

Responses to Terrorism

US PATRIOT Act, 2001

Under the Provide Appropriate Tools Required to Intercept and Obstruct Terrorism Act, immigrants in the USA are liable to detention and deportation if they provide otherwise lawful assistance to groups and organizations that may or may not have been officially designated as terrorists but are suspected of involvement in or sympathy with terrorist causes. Section 411 of the Act requires those accused to prove that they did not know and could not have known that their assistance would further terrorist activity, thereby reversing the conventional burden of proof.

UK Terrorism Acts, 2000 and 2006

Between 2001 and 2008, UK police forces stopped and searched over 180,000 people under section 44 of the 2000 Terrorism Act. Of these, only 255 individuals were subsequently charged on suspicion of terrorist-related activity. The 2006 Act expanded the definition of a terrorist offence to include "encouragement of terrorism", and extended the period of detention without charge from 14 to 28 days.

ALGERIA, 2007 At least 150 people were killed in a campaign by an al Qaida group.

MADRID, SPAIN, 2004 Bombs on four trains killed 191 people.

LONDON, UK, 2005 Four suicide bombers on public transport killed 52 people.

MOSCOW, RUSSIA, 2002 50 Chechen fighters held 700 theatre-goers hostage. Rescue raid by Russian forces killed Chechens and more than 100 hostages.

BESLAN, RUSSIA, 2004 Chechen fighters held children and parents hostage in school. When Russian security forces stormed the school, 336 hostages died, among them this woman's two granddaughters.

AFGHANISTAN, 2006– Taliban fighters used suicide and roadside bombs against NATO troops, Afghan civilians and security forces.

PAKISTAN, 2007 Bombs in Karachi killed 140 supporters of ex-Prime Minister Benazir Bhutto on her return from exile. In December she, and 28 supporters, were killed in Rawalpindi.

MUMBAI, INDIA, 2008 Terrorists attacked two luxury hotels in Mumbai, India and killed 166 people. A subsequent siege of both hotels resulted in Indian security forces killing all but one of the terrorists and releasing the remaining guests.

GUJARAT, INDIA, 2002 29 Hindu worshippers were killed by unknown gunmen.

BEIRUT, LEBANON, 2005 Bomb killed former Prime Minister Rafiq Hariri and 20 others.

RED SEA COAST, EGYPT Sharm el-Sheikh, 2005: 88 killed; Dahab, 2006: 23 killed.

ISRAEL and PALESTINIAN TERRITORIES Since 2000, Palestinian groups have used suicide bombings and rocket attacks against occupation by Israel, which has responded with targeted killings, rocket strikes and army offensives, including that against Hamas in the Gaza Strip in 2008–09, which killed 1,000 Palestinians, many of them children.

RIYADH, SAUDI ARABIA, 2003 Suicide bomber killed 26 in attack on western housing complex.

MOMBASA, KENYA, 2002 Al Qaida suicide bomb attack on hotel killed three Israelis and 10 Kenyans.

SRI LANKA, 1980s–2009 The Liberation Tigers of Tamil Eelam killed, among others, a president of Sri Lanka, a former Prime Minister of India, and 40 Sri Lankan politicians.

IRAQ, 2003– Al Qaida-inspired insurgents responded to the occupation of Iraq with suicide bombs and other devices, killing coalition forces, and thousands of Iraqi civilians and security forces.

BALI, INDONESIA, 2002 200 holidaymakers were killed by an al Qaida bomb attack.

UN Peacekeeping

UN peacekeeping missions make an important contribution to the protection of human rights by maintaining peace agreements and seeking to establish the conditions for a sustainable future in regions scarred by armed conflict.

UN peacekeepers are largely assembled from the armed forces of UN member states, although they also include engineers, political advisors and electoral officials. Their role is complex and, in some instances, controversial. UN peacekeepers are normally deployed to maintain an already established cessation of hostilities, and their mandate usually imposes strict limitations on their ability to proactively engage in military action. If hostilities reignite or are still ongoing, this restricted mandate may prevent UN peacekeepers from upholding the human rights – including the lives – of those they have been deployed to "protect".

The number of peace missions has increased markedly since the 1990s, mainly in response to outbreaks of intra-state conflict, such as those in central Africa, and the UN is struggling to raise the money and troops to support them. While it is the richer countries who provide the funds, the majority of peacekeeping missions are composed of forces from the poorer, developing-world societies.

...over **2,600 peacekeepers were killed** on duty between 1948 and mid-2009...

UN Peacekeeping Operations
Number of people committed to UN peacekeeping operations *end 2008*

- 1,000 or more
- 500 – 999
- 100 – 499
- fewer than 100
- none
- UN peacekeeping mission ongoing *June 2009*

The Massacre of Srebrenica
A woman mourns over the coffin of a body exhumed from a mass grave in Bosnia and Herzegovina. In July 1995, during the Bosnian War, Serb forces commanded by Ratko Mladic murdered 8,000 Bosnian Muslim boys and men from Srebrenica. The UN had passed two resolutions designating the town a "safe area", but 400 Dutch peacekeepers deployed to enforce UN resolutions were ordered by their commanding officer not to prevent the boys and men from being marched away. The International Criminal Tribunal for the former Yugoslavia later condemned the massacre as genocide.

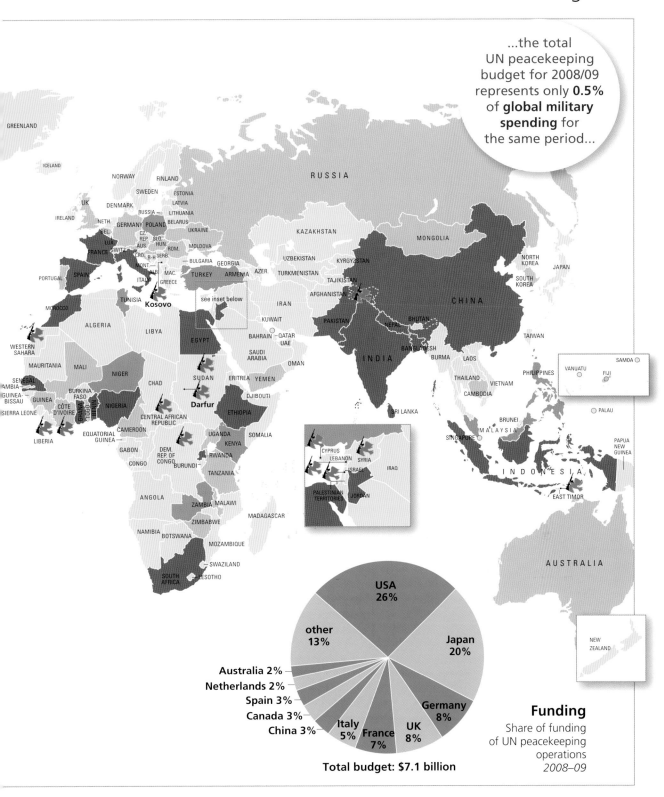

...the total UN peacekeeping budget for 2008/09 represents only **0.5%** of **global military spending** for the same period...

Funding

Share of funding of UN peacekeeping operations
2008–09

Total budget: $7.1 billion

USA 26%
Japan 20%
Germany 8%
UK 8%
France 7%
Italy 5%
China 3%
Canada 3%
Spain 3%
Netherlands 2%
Australia 2%
other 13%

Refugees, IDPs & Stateless

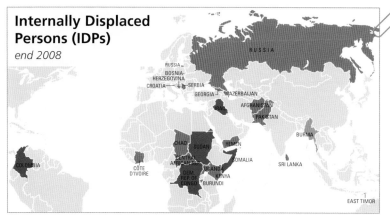

Internally Displaced Persons (IDPs)
end 2008

RUSSIA
BOSNIA-HERZEGOVINA
CROATIA
SERBIA
GEORGIA
AZERBAIJAN
IRAQ
AFGHANISTAN
PAKISTAN
BURMA
CHAD
SUDAN
YEMEN
CENTRAL AFRICAN REP.
UGANDA
SOMALIA
SRI LANKA
CÔTE D'IVOIRE
DEM. REP. OF CONGO
KENYA
BURUNDI
COLOMBIA
EAST TIMOR

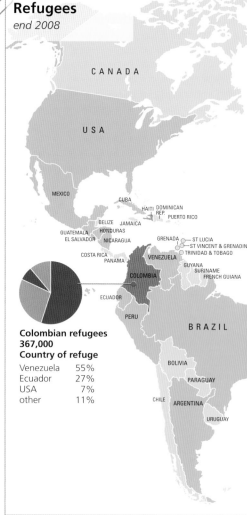

Refugees
end 2008

CANADA
USA
MEXICO
CUBA
HAITI
DOMINICAN REP.
PUERTO RICO
BELIZE
JAMAICA
GUATEMALA
HONDURAS
EL SALVADOR
NICARAGUA
GRENADA
ST LUCIA
ST VINCENT & GRENADINES
TRINIDAD & TOBAGO
COSTA RICA
PANAMA
VENEZUELA
GUYANA
SURINAME
FRENCH GUIANA
COLOMBIA
ECUADOR
PERU
BRAZIL
BOLIVIA
PARAGUAY
CHILE
ARGENTINA
URUGUAY

Colombian refugees
367,000
Country of refuge

Venezuela	55%
Ecuador	27%
USA	7%
other	11%

Refugees and IDPs are a barometer of political instability and continuing systematic persecution.

Their prevalence and geographical origin and distribution bears witness to the dramatically different conditions experienced by populations of industrialized and developing countries.

Refugees and internally displaced people (IDPs) are those forced to leave their homes or country as a result of armed conflict, political repression, persecution and systematic discrimination. Refugees are defined as those seeking political refuge and asylum outside their country of nationality, whereas IDPs have remained within their country of residence.

Worldwide, there are an estimated 15 million stateless people – those not recognized as citizens by any national authority. Typically, only citizens are able to access their fundamental rights, and the rights of stateless people are therefore in permanent jeopardy. According to the UNHCR, statelessness has several distinct causes, including discrimination against minority groups in nationality legislation, failure to include all residents in the body of citizens when a state becomes independent (state succession), and conflicts of laws between states.

The fundamental obstacles to achieving genuinely durable solutions to this particular human rights concern are continuing political instability and discrimination in those countries producing the highest numbers of refugees and IDPs and stateless peoples.

Refugees and IDPs

Official refugees, people in refugee-like situations and internally displaced people by country of origin
end 2008

▨	1 million or more
▨	100,000 – 999,999
▨	10,000 – 99,999
▨	1,000 – 9,999
▨	fewer than 1,000
▨	no data

What the law says...

The term "refugee" shall apply to any person who, owing to well-founded fear of being persecuted for reasons of race, religion, nationality, membership of a particular social group or political opinion, is outside the country of his nationality and is unable, or owing to such fear, is unwilling to avail himself of the protection of that country.

UN Convention Relating to the Status of Refugees, 1951, Article 1

Conflict & Migration

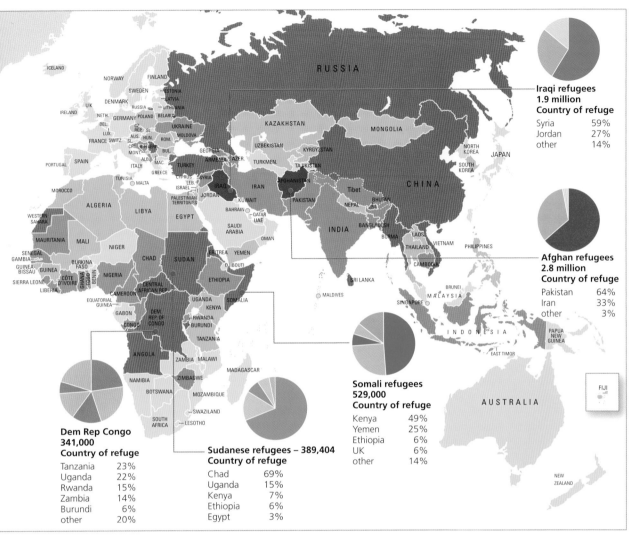

Iraqi refugees
1.9 million
Country of refuge

Syria	59%
Jordan	27%
other	14%

Afghan refugees
2.8 million
Country of refuge

Pakistan	64%
Iran	33%
other	3%

Somali refugees
529,000
Country of refuge

Kenya	49%
Yemen	25%
Ethiopia	6%
UK	6%
other	14%

Dem Rep Congo
341,000
Country of refuge

Tanzania	23%
Uganda	22%
Rwanda	15%
Zambia	14%
Burundi	6%
other	20%

Sudanese refugees – 389,404
Country of refuge

Chad	69%
Uganda	15%
Kenya	7%
Ethiopia	6%
Egypt	3%

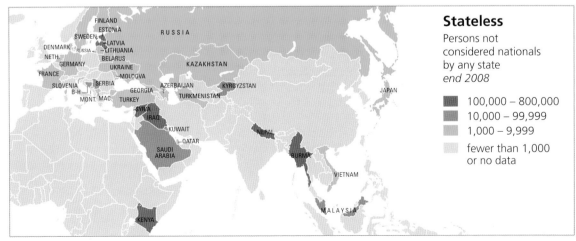

Stateless

Persons not
considered nationals
by any state
end 2008

- 100,000 – 800,000
- 10,000 – 99,999
- 1,000 – 9,999
- fewer than 1,000
  or no data

Part 5

Discrimination

The desire to counter formal inequality and discrimination is central to the moral DNA of the human rights project. We have fundamental human rights simply by virtue of being human: each individual's claim to human rights pre-exists all of those attributes, such as, for example, gender, race, ethnicity, religious conviction, national identity, or physical and psychological abilities, which distinguish individual human beings from each other. However, many human rights violations occur precisely because an individual's or community's identity has been targeted by others.

Human rights to protect against racial, ethnic and national discrimination have been recognized, and the right to be free from discrimination and persecution on grounds of religion has exerted a deep influence upon the historical development of human rights. More recently, people suffering from long-standing physical or psychological disabilities have received international recognition.

Despite these accomplishments, countless millions of people continue to suffer human rights violations on the basis of their identity. Many others also suffer from diminished opportunities. Racial and ethnic minorities face widespread discrimination across the globe. In some cases these forms of discrimination persist despite laws proscribing them; in other cases, no such legal mechanisms exist. Countless millions of people also suffer discrimination and the risk of injury or death as a consequence of seeking to practice a religion condemned by the prevailing majority. The effects of religious discrimination and prejudice are most pronounced where the state is based upon, and espouses, a majority religion.

Discrimination and inequality can also be found beyond the realm of those human rights comprehensively recognized by international human rights law. Foremost amongst these is discrimination on grounds of sexual identity and orientation. In many parts of the world today sexual minorities face systematic discrimination. Sexual acts between same-sex couples are illegal in many countries, and in some the maximum sentence for homosexuality is death.

CUBA: Transvestites in Havana, where attitudes towards sexual freedom are gradually relaxing.

Religious Freedom & Persecution

Despite predictions to the contrary, religious faith is a central feature of human life, with around 80 percent of people in the world professing allegiance to a religion.

For the vast majority of people, their religion is a central component of their identity. Indeed, with the demise of the strictly atheistic state socialist system and a resurgence of fundamentalist faith in some parts of the world, religion appears to exercise more influence on domestic and global politics than at any time during the past 100 years.

The diversity of faiths – from the world religions of Buddhism, Christianity, Hinduism, Islam and Judaism to indigenous, animistic, shamanistic religions, and newly emerging cults – and the inherent incompatibility of belief systems creates the potential for conflict and persecution. In many cases, the greatest threat to an individual's right to hold and profess a religious belief comes not from dogmatic secularists, but from religious communities that discriminate against and persecute members of adjacent minority religions.

Discrimination on the basis of religion is generally more likely to occur the more strongly a state formally adheres to an established religion. However, the atheistic state ideology in China also condemns many religious believers to systematic persecution. And a commitment to secularism on the part of some European states, most notably France, results in the limitation of religious expression in the public sphere.

What the law says...

Everyone shall have the right to freedom of thought, conscience and religion. This right shall include freedom to have or to adopt a religion or belief of his choice, and freedom, either individually or in community with others and in public or private, to manifest his religion or belief in worship, observance, practice and teaching.

International Covenant on Civil and Political Rights, 1966, Article 18

Constraints on Religious Freedom

Assessment by the CIRI Human Rights Dataset of government restrictions on freedom to practise religion and proselytize peacefully

- severe
- moderate
- practically absent
- no data

Christian Tigrinya women praying for peace at the orthodox cathedral in Eritrea. As adherents to a religious organization sanctioned by the government, they are free to worship. Thousands of others are not so fortunate.

Discrimination

FRANCE French law supports the state's secularist principles by restricting the expression of religious faith to places of worship and the home. The wearing of religious symbols is banned within state buildings, such as schools. While French law has been upheld in the European Court of Human Rights, it remains a source of considerable tension between the French state and resident Muslims.

IRAN The Islamic Republic adheres to the Shi'a Muslim doctrine, and Sunni Muslims, who are in the minority, face substantial discrimination from government authorities and the Shi'a community. The government regards the Baha'i faith, which originated in the country in 1844, as an heretical Islamic faith. Baha'i are prohibited from teaching and practising their faith, and suffer arbitrary arrests and confiscation of property.

UZBEKISTAN The separation of church and state is enshrined within the constitution, but the 1998 Religion Law restricts many rights to members of registered religious groups. Some (particularly Islamic) groups are routinely refused registration and are effectively outlawed. Jews, Russian Orthodox, and other ethnic religious communities may practise their religion so long as they do not criticize the government or proselytize.

CHINA Although the world's five main religions are tolerated, their practice is restricted. Religious organizations are monitored to ensure that they do not disrupt public order or interfere with the educational system, and are not subject to foreign domination. Underground Catholic bishops face repression for their allegiance to the Vatican, and Protestants who worship in unofficial "house" churches have been persecuted. In Xinjiang, authorities confiscated the passports of 2,000 Uighur Muslims due to participate in a Hajj pilgrimage in 2009.

SAUDI ARABIA Non-Muslims and Muslims who do not follow the government's interpretation of Islam continue to face significant discrimination and violent assault by the religious police. Saudi textbooks contain intolerant statements towards Shi'a, Ismailis, Jews, Christians, and those of other faiths. Some foreign workers have been arrested for practising their faith. Conversion by a Muslim to another faith is considered apostasy, a crime punishable by death.

ERITREA Following a 2002 decree, the government closed all religious facilities not belonging to the Eritrean Orthodox Church, the Catholic Church, the Evangelical Church of Eritrea, and Islam. Other groups, such as the Pentecostals, Jehovah's Witnesses and reformists within the Eritrean Orthodox Church were harassed, detained, tortured and even killed. In 2009, over 3,000 religious detainees continued to be held without due process and in extreme conditions.

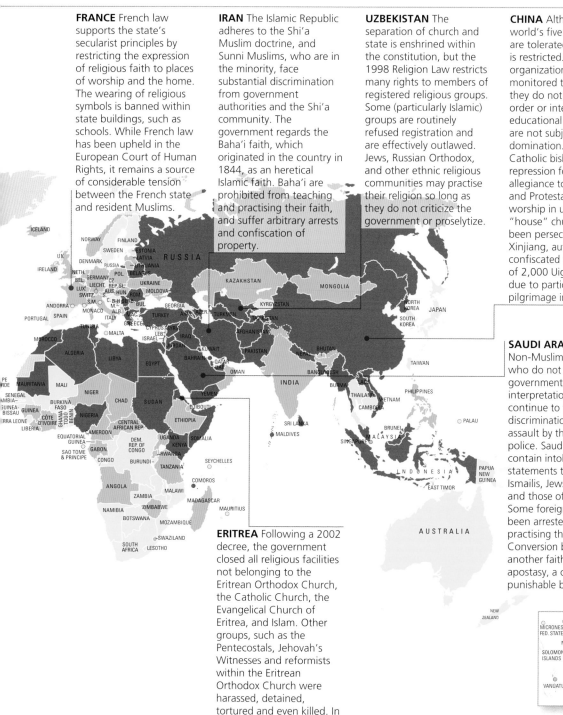

Minorities

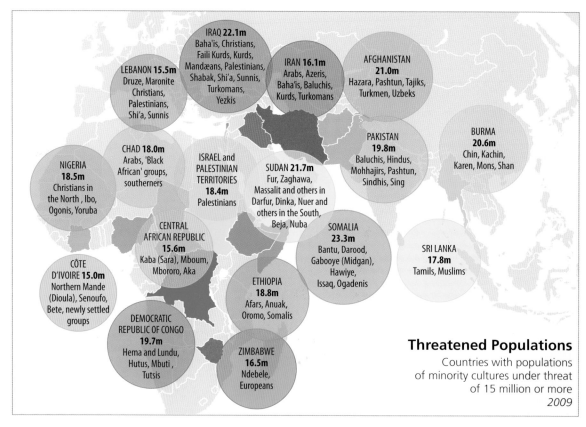

IRAQ 22.1m
Baha'is, Christians, Faili Kurds, Kurds, Mandæans, Palestinians, Shabak, Shi'a, Sunnis, Turkomans, Yezkis

LEBANON 15.5m
Druze, Maronite Christians, Palestinians, Shi'a, Sunnis

IRAN 16.1m
Arabs, Azeris, Baha'is, Baluchis, Kurds, Turkomans

AFGHANISTAN 21.0m
Hazara, Pashtun, Tajiks, Turkmen, Uzbeks

PAKISTAN 19.8m
Baluchis, Hindus, Mohhajirs, Pashtun, Sindhis, Sing

BURMA 20.6m
Chin, Kachin, Karen, Mons, Shan

NIGERIA 18.5m
Christians in the North, Ibo, Ogonis, Yoruba

CHAD 18.0m
Arabs, 'Black African' groups, southerners

ISRAEL and PALESTINIAN TERRITORIES 18.4m
Palestinians

SUDAN 21.7m
Fur, Zaghawa, Massalit and others in Darfur, Dinka, Nuer and others in the South, Beja, Nuba

SOMALIA 23.3m
Bantu, Darood, Gabooye (Midgan), Hawiye, Issaq, Ogadenis

SRI LANKA 17.8m
Tamils, Muslims

CENTRAL AFRICAN REPUBLIC 15.6m
Kaba (Sara), Mboum, Mbororo, Aka

CÔTE D'IVOIRE 15.0m
Northern Mande (Dioula), Senoufo, Bete, newly settled groups

ETHIOPIA 18.8m
Afars, Anuak, Oromo, Somalis

DEMOCRATIC REPUBLIC OF CONGO 19.7m
Hema and Lundu, Hutus, Mbuti, Tutsis

ZIMBABWE 16.5m
Ndebele, Europeans

Threatened Populations
Countries with populations of minority cultures under threat of 15 million or more
2009

The populations of few, if any, countries comprise a homogenous community. Minorities exist in almost all countries, and many suffer persecution, oppression and systematic discrimination.

One of the worst ongoing campaigns violating the rights of a minority is taking place in the Darfur region of Sudan, where Black African Muslims are being targeted by government-backed Arab Janjaweed militia. In 2004, the US government described this as constituting a form of genocide. Burma's military regime is also conducting systematic campaigns against at least four ethnic communities: the Karen, the Shans, the Rohingya, and the Zomis.

Minority rights violations are not restricted to conflict-ridden, politically unstable regions of the world. The Roma have long been subject to conditions of discrimination and inequality within the borders of the European Union. Similarly, ethnic Koreans continue to experience discrimination and formal inequality within Japan. Many indigenous communities in North America and Australasia also argue that the conditions they face constitute a severe violation of their right to maintain their distinctive traditions and cultures.

Amidst the wealth and infrastructural development of countries such as Australia, Canada, New Zealand and the USA are to be found indigenous communities with mortality and morbidity statistics which, in some cases, rival those found in Sub-Saharan Africa.

Protection
Human rights instruments intended to protect ethnic, national, religious, indigenous or linguistic minorities

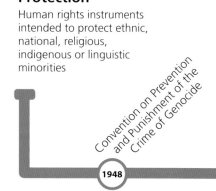

Convention on Prevention and Punishment of the Crime of Genocide

1948

Threatened Cultures

Selected examples
2009

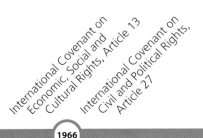

CROATIA, GREECE, ITALY The **Roma** people have been subject to consistent discrimination by public officials, and are the target of public protest. In Italy, a decree law was introduced in 2008 that allowed authorities to expel EU citizens on grounds of public security. Within two weeks of its introduction, 177 Romanian citizens of Roma origin had been expelled.

SAUDI ARABIA The **Shi'a** Muslims are the largest minority group, and are viewed by the Saudi regime as potentially subversive. They have no rights to free expression, face employment discrimination and officially sanctioned religious discrimination. Numerous Shi'a clerics have been detained and held without charge or access to legal representation.

BURMA The **Karen** occupy an area along the Burma–Thailand border. They are a distinct, although heterogeneous, ethnic community that has suffered long-standing repression. Some sections of the community have been engaged in armed conflict with the Burmese military since 1949 in an attempt to secure independence.

AUSTRALIA The **Aboriginal** communities have experienced consistent discrimination for many decades. This has involved the loss of tribal lands, the forced removal of children, and levels of educational and health facilities below those of other Australians. In 2006, the average life expectancy of Aboriginal males was 56 years, compared with 77 for all Australian males.

International Covenant on Economic, Social and Cultural Rights, Article 13

International Covenant on Civil and Political Rights, Article 27

International Labour Organisation, Convention 169

Declaration on the Rights of Persons Belonging to National or Ethnic, Religious or Linguistic Minorities

Declaration on the Rights of Indigenous Peoples

1966   **1989** **1992**   **2007**

Racism

Real progress has been made in the area of racial equality, but racist attitudes and overt forms of discrimination continue in many parts of the world today.

Racism is a truly global phenomenon, evident in industrialized and developing countries alike. Within some countries, racist policies are formalized in domestic law. In many others, racist beliefs and practises are less overt, but still have a detrimental effect on the targeted groups – restricting their life opportunities, making them feel insecure and leading to lowered life expectancy.

Arguably the single greatest success for the global human rights movement in the past 20 years was the demise of the apartheid system in South Africa. More recently, the election of the first African-American to the Presidency of the USA has sent a strong and positive message around the world.

USA Federal legislation prohibits racism, but many African-Americans continue to suffer from economic inequality and exposure to crime. While a discrepancy in life expectancy between white Americans and African-Americans has been slowly diminishing, the gap remains. By comparison with whites, African-Americans are twice as likely to be unemployed, three times as likely to live in poverty, and six times as likely to be imprisoned.

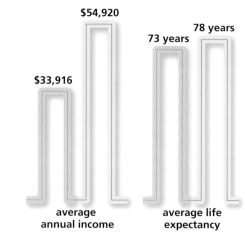

$54,920

78 years

73 years

$33,916

Inequality in USA

Comparison of average annual income and life expectancy
2007

▦ African-American
— white

| average annual income | average life expectancy |

What the law says...

States Parties condemn racial discrimination and undertake to pursue by all appropriate means and without delay a policy of eliminating racial discrimination in all its forms and promoting understanding among all races.

International Convention on the Elimination of All Forms of Racial Discrimination, 1966, Article 2 (1)

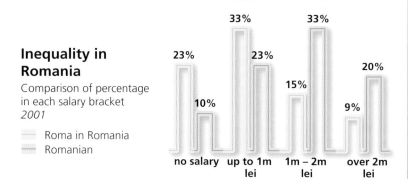

Inequality in Romania

Comparison of percentage in each salary bracket
2001

▦ Roma in Romania
▦ Romanian

23% **33%** **23%** **33%** **15%** **20%** **10%** **9%**

| no salary | up to 1m lei | 1m – 2m lei | over 2m lei |

EUROPE Racist attitudes and practices remain in the EU, despite the commitment of its members to eradicating racism through anti-discrimination legislation that secures equal rights for all.

In France, the openly racist Front National polled 16% of the vote in 2002, and even ostensibly moderate politicians are prepared to discuss the idea of "national preference", whereby certain jobs would be reserved for French nationals.

In Romania, 10% of people openly express racist views, such as statements that Black and Chinese people should not live there, while 66% assert that Roma people should be prevented from leaving the country because they damage the image of Romania. Roughly half of Romanians support birth control to limit the size of the Roma population.

In the UK, people of African-Caribbean origin were six times more likely to be stopped and searched, and those of Asian origin twice as likely, than were white people in 2005.

INDIA Although the constitution proclaims equality for all, the predominant religion, Hinduism, is characterized by a caste system that determines people's access to public and private spaces, education, healthcare, occupation and even marriage partners. Those of the lowest caste, the so-called Dalits, continue to suffer discrimination and systematic abuse, including extrajudicial killings and considerable rates of sexual abuse and rape. In 2008, six people were charged under the Scheduled Castes (Prevention) Act for piercing the eyes of a Dalit man as punishment for his relationship with one of their relatives.

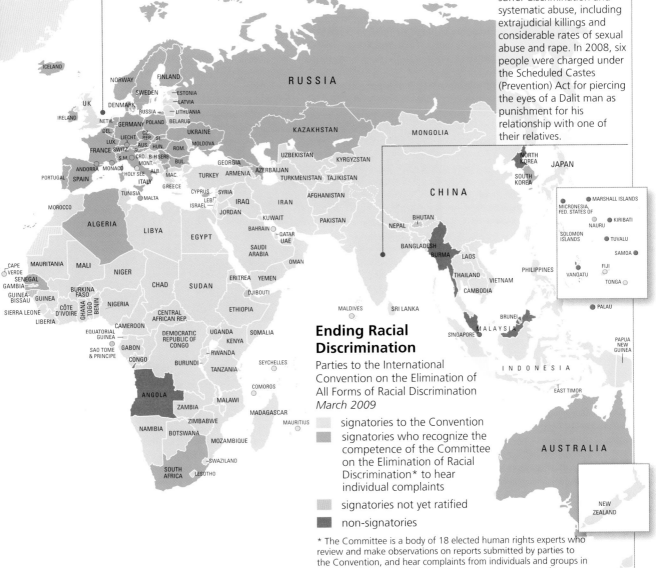

Ending Racial Discrimination

Parties to the International Convention on the Elimination of All Forms of Racial Discrimination
March 2009

- signatories to the Convention
- signatories who recognize the competence of the Committee on the Elimination of Racial Discrimination* to hear individual complaints
- signatories not yet ratified
- non-signatories

* The Committee is a body of 18 elected human rights experts who review and make observations on reports submitted by parties to the Convention, and hear complaints from individuals and groups in countries that recognize the Committee's competence to do so.

Disabilities & Mental Health

People with both physical and mental disabilities have been abused and discriminated against for centuries, and this continues across the world today.

The level of abuse varies, but includes social stigmatization and incarceration. Disabled people may experience employment discrimination, be denied access to benefits and financial assistance, and find their access to public spaces restricted. Mental health patients are frequently shackled, beaten or confined to "cage beds". These conditions are worst in the poorer regions of the world.

Progress has, however, been achieved in recognizing the rights of the disabled, with the adoption in 2008 of the UN Convention on the Rights of Persons with Disabilities. It aims to achieve a "paradigm shift" in the understanding of, and approach to, people with disabilities, stating that disabled people are fully entitled to equality of respect and the inherent dignity of all human beings. It establishes that the rights of disabled people comprise both the right to be free from discrimination and the right to receive adequate healthcare.

Wholesale discrimination and human rights abuses continue to occur, but the Convention may be credited with establishing a legal benchmark for determining what the disabled are entitled to by right, rather than as a result of charity.

What the law says...

Persons with disabilities include those who have long-term physical, mental, intellectual or sensory impairments which in interaction with various barriers may hinder their full and effective participation in society on an equal basis with others.

Convention on the Rights of Persons with Disabilities, 2006, Article 1

In Sierra Leone, many children had their limbs amputated by insurgents during the civil war. Lahai has a wheelchair to help him to get around, but neither he, nor his brother, who helps care for him, are able to go to school.

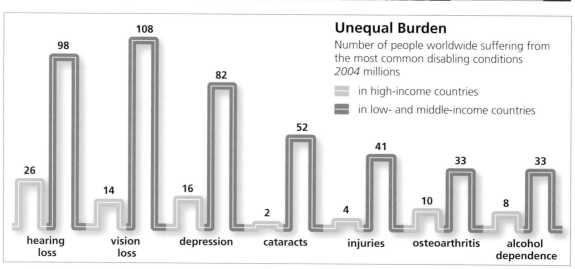

Unequal Burden

Number of people worldwide suffering from the most common disabling conditions
2004 millions

▬ in high-income countries

▬ in low- and middle-income countries

	hearing loss	vision loss	depression	cataracts	injuries	osteoarthritis	alcohol dependence
high-income	26	14	16	2	4	10	8
low/middle-income	98	108	82	52	41	33	33

Discrimination

Disability Benefits

Percentage of countries in each WHO region
where disability benefits are available
2005

More than three-quarters of countries have passed laws that
seek to protect the disabled against formal discrimination,
but widespread informal discrimination occurs because
inadequate services and inhospitable environments prevent
disabled people from fully participating in society. In
countries where a lack of resources restricts the provision of
services, disabled people are often cared for by family
members, putting them under increased financial strain.

46% Africa
91% Americas
86% Eastern Med.
100% Europe
82% South-East Asia
65% Western Pacific
78% World

...the WHO
estimates that
15% of people
worldwide
are **severely
disabled**...

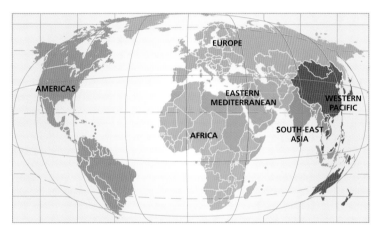

EUROPE
AMERICAS
EASTERN MEDITERRANEAN
WESTERN PACIFIC
AFRICA
SOUTH-EAST ASIA

Mental Health Policies

Percentage of countries in each WHO region with policy
on improving mental health
2005

Absence of a concerted policy often leads to disorganized
and inefficient provision of services, and a general lack of
accountability, exacerbating the poor conditions experienced
by people with mental disorders.

Community Care

Percentage of countries in
each WHO region providing community care
for people with mental disorders
2005

Although services exist in over two-thirds of countries, these
may be restricted to only a few areas, as is the case in China
and India. The absence of effective services results in people
with mental disorders being incarcerated in institutions,
many of which offer little or no effective therapeutic regime.

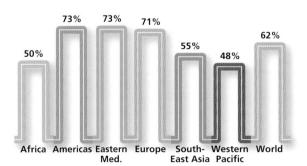

50% Africa
73% Americas
73% Eastern Med.
71% Europe
55% South-East Asia
48% Western Pacific
62% World

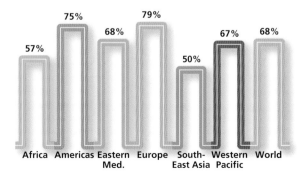

57% Africa
75% Americas
68% Eastern Med.
79% Europe
50% South-East Asia
67% Western Pacific
68% World

Sexual Freedom

A right to sexual freedom is yet to be formally recognized as a fundamental human right.

Sexual relations between same-sex partners remain deeply controversial in many countries. For some cultures and religions male homosexuality in particular is considered a violation of cultural traditions and sacred tenets, and the demand that other cultures respect this position has constituted a powerful obstacle to establishing sexual freedom as a fundamental human right.

Many countries continue to criminalize same-sex relations, and in a small number the ultimate punishment is death. Even where the penalty is less severe, the threat of family or community rejection or recrimination often prompts sexual minorities to lead double lives, making them vulnerable to police blackmail and extortion. They may also face arbitrary arrest and detention, physical attacks, and discrimination in areas of employment, education and access to healthcare.

Prejudices remain even within societies that underwent the so-called "sexual revolution" of the 1960s, and where same-sex sexual relations are legal. However, an increasing number of countries are passing laws allowing same-sex marriage and civil unions, although laws can be overturned, as occurred in California, USA in 2008.

Choice of sexual partner is a feature of the lives of many adults, and is an essential aspect of the right to individual liberty. A respect for human rights necessitates a commitment to the ideal of personal equality. Cultural, religious and legal sanctions for same-sex relations constitute a flagrant violation of these principles, and are a form of systematic discrimination. Despite the force of the argument, however, sexual freedom remains a human right yet to be satisfactorily realized.

Legislation has been introduced in a number of countries and US states giving same-sex couples similar rights to opposite-sex partners in civil partnerships and marriage.

Legislation on Homosexuality

- illegal
- legal
- unclear
- no data
- ● death penalty is maximum sentence for same-sex sexual acts

CANADA

USA

MEXICO
BAHAMAS
CUBA
DOMINICAN REP.
JAMAICA HAITI PUERTO RICO
BELIZE ST KITTS & NEVIS ANTIGUA & BARBUDA
GUATEMALA HONDURAS
EL SALVADOR DOMINICA
NICARAGUA GRENADA ST LUCIA
BARBADOS
COSTA RICA ST VINCENT & GRENADINES
PANAMA VENEZUELA TRINIDAD & TOBAGO
GUYANA
COLOMBIA SURINAME
ECUADOR
PERU
BOLIVIA
CHILE PARAGUAY
ARGENTINA
URUGUAY

CARIBBEAN The Caribbean islands have some of the harshest sentences for homosexual acts. In Barbados and Guyana a conviction carries a maximum life sentence. In Trinidad and Tobago, it is 25 years. In 2000, the British government met with significant opposition to its demand that laws against homosexuality in its Caribbean territories be repealed.

In January 2008, a group of friends were attacked in their home in Jamaica by more than 15 men wielding knives and machetes and shouting anti-gay slogans.

Increasing Recognition

The introduction of countrywide legislation formalizing same-sex partnerships
1989–2009

Denmark
1989

Sweden
1994

Hungary
1995

Iceland, Norway
1996

Netherlands
1997

France
1999

Vermont – first US state to offer same-sex civil union
2000

Discrimination

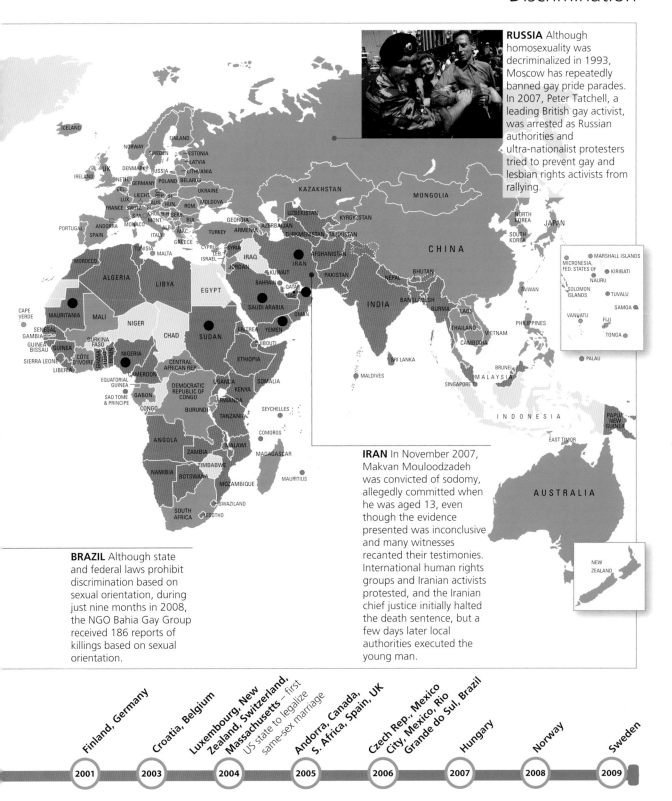

RUSSIA Although homosexuality was decriminalized in 1993, Moscow has repeatedly banned gay pride parades. In 2007, Peter Tatchell, a leading British gay activist, was arrested as Russian authorities and ultra-nationalist protesters tried to prevent gay and lesbian rights activists from rallying.

IRAN In November 2007, Makvan Mouloodzadeh was convicted of sodomy, allegedly committed when he was aged 13, even though the evidence presented was inconclusive and many witnesses recanted their testimonies. International human rights groups and Iranian activists protested, and the Iranian chief justice initially halted the death sentence, but a few days later local authorities executed the young man.

BRAZIL Although state and federal laws prohibit discrimination based on sexual orientation, during just nine months in 2008, the NGO Bahia Gay Group received 186 reports of killings based on sexual orientation.

2001	2003	2004	2005	2006	2007	2008	2009
Finland, Germany	Croatia, Belgium	Luxembourg, New Zealand, Switzerland, **Massachusetts** – first US state to legalize same-sex marriage	Andorra, Canada, S. Africa, Spain, UK	Czech Rep., Mexico City, Mexico, Rio Grande do Sul, Brazil	Hungary	Norway	Sweden

Part 6

Women's Rights

Women and girls comprise at least half of the world's population, but this numerical parity is not reflected in the respective human rights conditions of men and women. Across the world, women continue to face direct and indirect forms of inequality and discrimination.

Despite the fact that women have secured formal legal equality across the developed world, in many of these countries women continue to suffer from the effects of indirect inequality in the form of lower wages, rape and domestic violence, and cultural stereotypes which adversely affect the health and well-being of many women. The systematic violation of women's rights is most evident, however, in countries that have refused to recognize the equal standing of women. Many countries continue to deny women the vote or an opportunity to participate in the civil and public life of their communities. Similarly, countless millions of women are denied the right to own property.

Women's control over their own bodies is also severely restricted across many parts of the globe in the form of wholesale denial of access to abortion or forms of reproductive health. This also extends to the practice of female genital mutilation, which has irreversible effects upon many women's sexuality and health. Across the globe the sex industry has served to expose women to severe restrictions of their human rights and, in some cases, women are effectively enslaved within demeaning, degrading and even life-threatening conditions.

Women's human rights continue to suffer from the combined effects of state-sanctioned policies and laws, the persistence of overly restrictive cultural stereotypes and expectations, poverty and destitution, and deep-rooted cultural traditions and practices, the principal effect of which would appear to be the perpetuation of unequal power relations between men and women.

UK: Demonstrators in London on a march organized by Million Women Rise.

Women's Civil Rights

The systematic denial and restriction of women's civil rights across the world remains one of the central challenges to the human rights movement.

All human beings are entitled to the exercise of their fundamental human rights regardless of gender. In reality, women continue to face wholesale discrimination. Pervasive forms of inequality between men and women are apparent in such areas as women's right to divorce and own property, the imposition of formal dress codes, and their right to move freely within the private and public spheres.

In some countries, discrimination is explicit, and consists of restrictions placed on women on the basis of established legal, social, and religious tenets. Elsewhere, discrimination takes a less overt form, but is embedded in cultural attitudes that contribute to women's lower socio-economic opportunities, and may even have a detrimental effect on their health and well-being as they strive to conform to stereotypical images of female beauty.

The Beijing Declaration of 1995 reasserted the United Nations' commitment to establishing full gender equality. It identified several areas of critical concern, including the disproportionate impact of poverty on women, inequality in respect of access to healthcare and education, violence inflicted on women in the domestic sphere, and the damaging effects of persistent gender stereotyping of women and girls.

CEDAW

The UN Convention on the Elimination of All Forms of Discrimination against Women, 1979 (CEDAW) is the principal international legal instrument for the protection of women's rights. Most countries have signed and ratified it, but as of July 2009 the USA was still to ratify, and Iran, Nauru, Palau, Somalia, Sudan and Tonga had not signed. Over 65 of the signatory states have, however, entered "reservations" that exempt them from specific legal obligations, such as those on domestic and family relations within marriage (Egypt), divorce (Syria), equality of opportunities for women in public office (Israel), and the elimination of traditional forms of discriminatory practices (Niger and Singapore), thereby revealing their formal position on women's equality.

Women's Rights

CIRI Index
2009

- no equality of employment with men
- some equality measures but not effectively enforced
- some equality measures but low level of discrimination
- near equality of employment with men
- no data

✗ voting rights unequal to those of men

✘ significant inequality in civil rights

Women and Poverty

Percentage of families living below the official poverty line in the USA
2006

- all families
- female-headed families

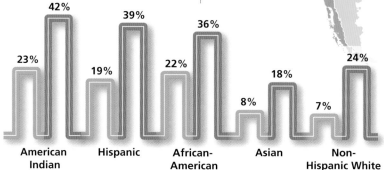

	American Indian	Hispanic	African-American	Asian	Non-Hispanic White
all families	23%	19%	22%	8%	7%
female-headed families	42%	39%	36%	18%	24%

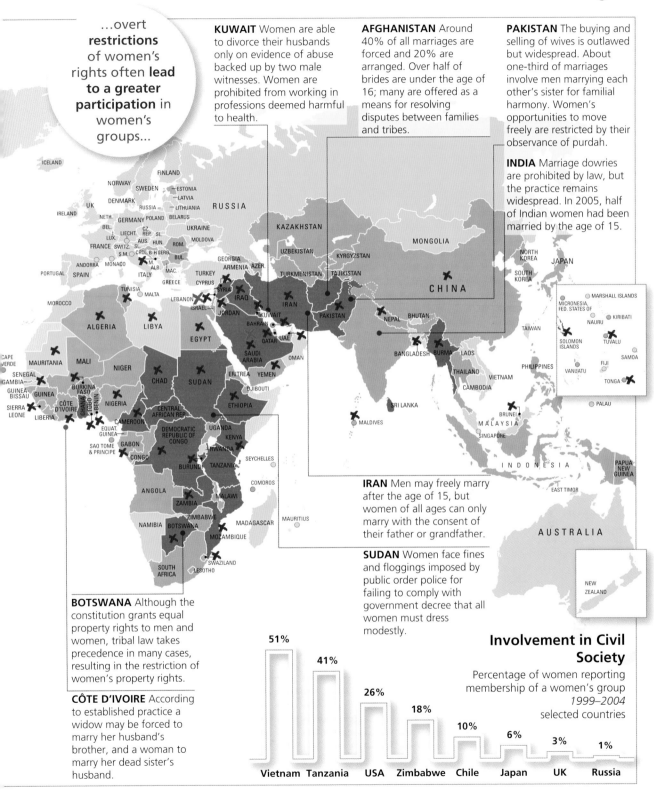

...overt **restrictions** of women's rights often **lead to a greater participation** in women's groups...

KUWAIT Women are able to divorce their husbands only on evidence of abuse backed up by two male witnesses. Women are prohibited from working in professions deemed harmful to health.

AFGHANISTAN Around 40% of all marriages are forced and 20% are arranged. Over half of brides are under the age of 16; many are offered as a means for resolving disputes between families and tribes.

PAKISTAN The buying and selling of wives is outlawed but widespread. About one-third of marriages involve men marrying each other's sister for familial harmony. Women's opportunities to move freely are restricted by their observance of purdah.

INDIA Marriage dowries are prohibited by law, but the practice remains widespread. In 2005, half of Indian women had been married by the age of 15.

IRAN Men may freely marry after the age of 15, but women of all ages can only marry with the consent of their father or grandfather.

SUDAN Women face fines and floggings imposed by public order police for failing to comply with government decree that all women must dress modestly.

BOTSWANA Although the constitution grants equal property rights to men and women, tribal law takes precedence in many cases, resulting in the restriction of women's property rights.

CÔTE D'IVOIRE According to established practice a widow may be forced to marry her husband's brother, and a woman to marry her dead sister's husband.

Involvement in Civil Society

Percentage of women reporting membership of a women's group *1999–2004* selected countries

Vietnam	Tanzania	USA	Zimbabwe	Chile	Japan	UK	Russia
51%	41%	26%	18%	10%	6%	3%	1%

Domestic Violence

The stark reality for many women across the world is that their right to life and security is most at risk not directly from state authorities but within the home and from their intimate partners.

Domestic violence ranges from psychological abuse and intimidation to physical assault, maiming and even death. While some violations of women's rights are more pronounced in some parts of the world than others, domestic violence is a truly global phenomenon. It occurs in all countries, and cuts across otherwise significant differences between women such as social class, economic prosperity, ethnic identity, and religious conviction.

State and social attitudes have a strong influence on policies to combat domestic violence. While the state does not practise domestic violence, the willingness to recognize the phenomenon as a human rights violation, rather than as a criminal assault, plays an important role in the establishment of public institutions charged with seeking to prevent domestic violence from occurring in the first place.

Social attitudes are also important in determining how domestic violence is evaluated and how perpetrators and victims are perceived. So-called "honour killings", in which men kill female family members deemed to have brought shame on the family by having sexual relations (even against their will) outside marriage are, in some countries, considered lesser crimes than the murder of an unrelated woman. And many women appear to accept that the marriage bond over-rides their human rights and entitles their husband to exercise violence towards them.

What the UN says...

"Violence against women and girls continues unabated in every continent, country and culture. It takes a devastating toll on women's lives, on their families, and on society as a whole. Most societies prohibit such violence – yet the reality is that too often, it is covered up or tacitly condoned."

Ban Ki-Moon (UN Secretary-General), 8 March 2007

Women under Attack

Violent attacks on women by intimate partners or family members
2000–09

■ honour killings regularly occur
  murders also occur

USA At least 20% of women are estimated to have been physically abused by their partners or ex-partners

HAITI Criminal law excuses a man from killing his wife if she has committed adultery.

ECUADOR

BRAZIL

Women's Views

Percentage of women who think it acceptable for a husband to beat his wife for one or more specific reasons: burning food, arguing with him, going out without telling him, neglecting the children, refusing sex
2004 selected countries

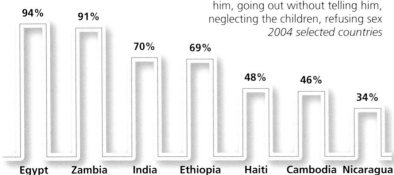

94%	91%	70%	69%	48%	46%	34%
Egypt	Zambia	India	Ethiopia	Haiti	Cambodia	Nicaragua

TURKEY A mother holds up a photo of her son, who killed his sister because she had "lost her honour" after being raped by her uncle. The Turkish government and judiciary have been criticized by Amnesty International for their failure to act over violence against women.

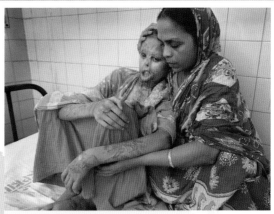

BANGLADESH Domestic violence is estimated to affect at least 50% of all adult women, many of these being related to dowry disputes. Acid attacks, such as that suffered by the young woman shown here with her mother, are particularly common, and can lead to disfigurement and blindness.

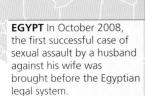

NETHERLANDS

MONTENEGRO

SERBIA

ITALY ALBANIA

LEBANON SYRIA

ISRAEL IRAQ IRAN AFGHANISTAN

MOROCCO

PALESTINIAN
TERRITORIES KUWAIT

INDIA

YEMEN

UGANDA

PAKISTAN So-called "honour killings" are widespread. In 2008, there were 21 reported cases of women being doused in kerosene and set alight. A 2005 law allows financial negotiations to lead to a lessening or dropping of charges for the murder of wives or daughters accused of dishonouring the family.

EGYPT In October 2008, the first successful case of sexual assault by a husband against his wife was brought before the Egyptian legal system.

ETHIOPIA Nearly 60% of women surveyed have been subjected to physical or sexual violence by an intimate partner during their lifetime. A separate survey found that most women believed that a man had a right to beat his wife.

JORDAN Between 15 and 20 women each year are killed in the name of family honour. Their murderers have typically received prison sentences of less than a year. Advocacy groups have long campaigned for a change of attitude and for heavier sentences, and in 2008 a man was jailed for more than 7 years for killing his sister.

SWAZILAND Over 60% of men believe it reasonable to beat their wives.

Rape

Rape constitutes a fundamental violation of the victim's human right to personal security. Like domestic violence, rape is a truly global phenomenon.

While there are incidences of male-on-male rape, the vast majority of the victims of rape are women, the perpetrators men. Rape is recognized as a crime across the world, but a number of factors render the gathering of reliable statistics on it very difficult.

There is a widely acknowledged problem of under-reporting, with many victims reluctant to go to the police, or even tell family members. Various factors account for this: social stigma, difficulties in securing a conviction and even the prospect, as in Afghanistan, that an unsuccessful prosecution is likely to result in the woman being charged for adultery if the perpetrator claims that she consented to sexual intercourse.

In some countries, the rape of a woman by her husband is perfectly legal and considered part of the man's conjugal rights. This category of rape will not appear in national criminal databases.

Rape is systematically used, throughout the world, as a way of subjugating civilian populations. It was eventually designated as a prosecutable war crime in the Rome Treaty of 1998.

> ...**one woman in five** will become a **victim of rape or attempted rape** in her lifetime...

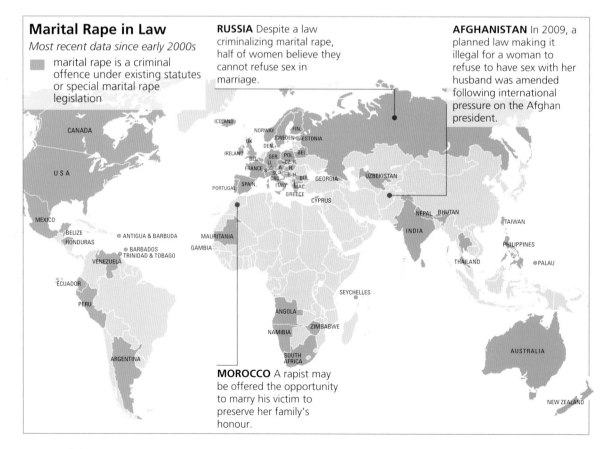

Marital Rape in Law

Most recent data since early 2000s

marital rape is a criminal offence under existing statutes or special marital rape legislation

RUSSIA Despite a law criminalizing marital rape, half of women believe they cannot refuse sex in marriage.

AFGHANISTAN In 2009, a planned law making it illegal for a woman to refuse to have sex with her husband was amended following international pressure on the Afghan president.

MOROCCO A rapist may be offered the opportunity to marry his victim to preserve her family's honour.

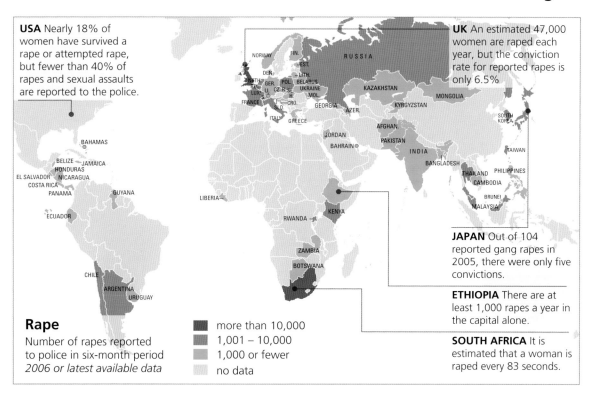

USA Nearly 18% of women have survived a rape or attempted rape, but fewer than 40% of rapes and sexual assaults are reported to the police.

UK An estimated 47,000 women are raped each year, but the conviction rate for reported rapes is only 6.5%

JAPAN Out of 104 reported gang rapes in 2005, there were only five convictions.

ETHIOPIA There are at least 1,000 rapes a year in the capital alone.

SOUTH AFRICA It is estimated that a woman is raped every 83 seconds.

Rape

Number of rapes reported to police in six-month period
2006 or latest available data

- more than 10,000
- 1,001 – 10,000
- 1,000 or fewer
- no data

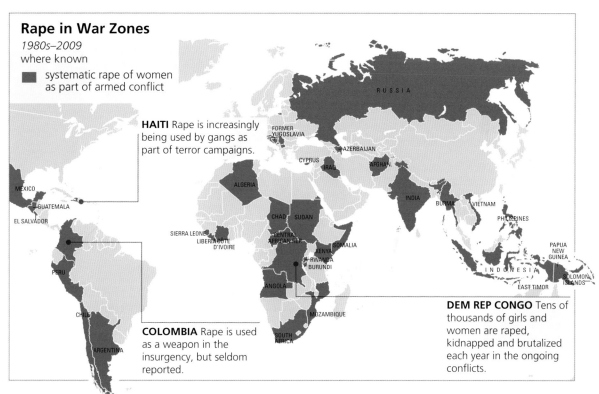

Rape in War Zones

1980s–2009
where known

- systematic rape of women as part of armed conflict

HAITI Rape is increasingly being used by gangs as part of terror campaigns.

COLOMBIA Rape is used as a weapon in the insurgency, but seldom reported.

DEM REP CONGO Tens of thousands of girls and women are raped, kidnapped and brutalized each year in the ongoing conflicts.

Right to Choose

A woman's right to choose whether to continue with a pregnancy remains embroiled in political and moral controversy throughout the world.

No human rights instrument grants women the right to an abortion, or even access to effective forms of contraception, and laws prohibiting abortion are not necessarily deemed contrary to human rights law.

Human rights rest heavily on the ideal of individual liberty. A strong argument can be made that the exercise of a woman's liberty must extend to an event as significant as becoming pregnant and choosing to terminate the pregnancy, and the absence of a distinct and specific human right in this area is perceived by many as an undue restriction upon that liberty.

A parallel argument can be made for a woman's human right to the highest attainable standard of healthcare. This is particularly an issue in those parts of the world where contraception is largely restricted or unavailable. The prevalence of HIV/AIDS among women in parts of Africa and Latin America is directly related to the lack of available contraception. Similarly, many women are exposed to unsafe abortions as a consequence of its legal proscription in some countries.

In spite of such arguments, women's reproductive rights remain subject to regulation and restriction in many parts of the world. Ironically, in some countries where abortion is prohibited it is frequently used to get rid of unwanted girl babies, who, in some cultures, are less highly valued than sons.

...**26% of people** live in a country where **abortion is prohibited**...

Access to Contraception
2007

20% or more of married women would like to limit childbearing but do not use any contraceptive device or technique

Legal Status of Abortion
2007

- illegal or severely restricted to saving woman's life
- illegal except to save life or preserve the health of woman and/or if the foetus is impaired
- legal for social or economic reasons
- legal on request but usually with gestational limits
- unclear

...around **70,000 women die** each year from complications associated with illegal abortions...

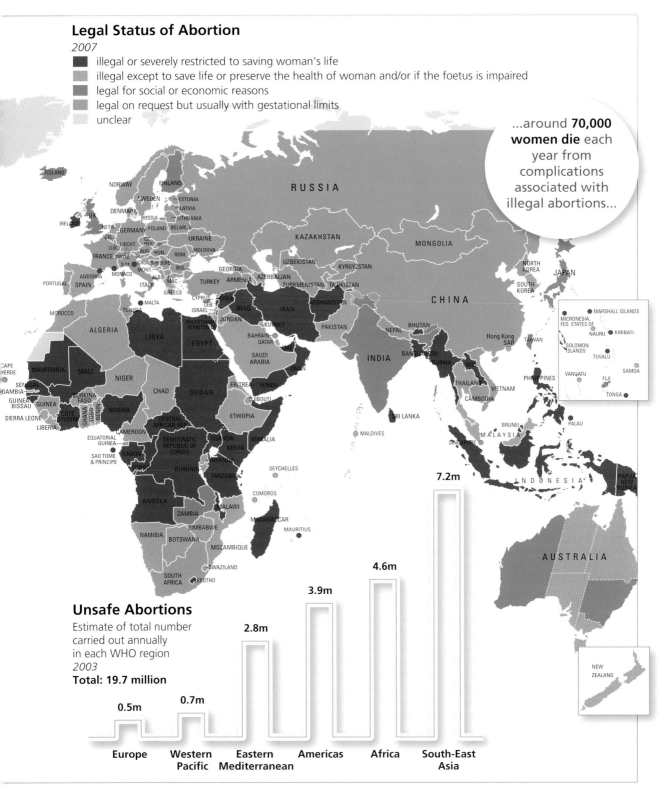

Unsafe Abortions
Estimate of total number carried out annually in each WHO region
2003
Total: 19.7 million

Europe	Western Pacific	Eastern Mediterranean	Americas	Africa	South-East Asia
0.5m	0.7m	2.8m	3.9m	4.6m	7.2m

Female Genital Mutilation

From a human rights perspective, the practice of female genital mutilation (FGM) is considered a violent act with significant and long-lasting consequences for its victims.

FGM is particularly prevalent in areas of the Middle East and Sub-Saharan Africa and raises interesting human rights issues. It is a long-established feature of many communities' way of life, and a commitment to human rights is typically associated with an acceptance of cultural diversity and the principle of self-determination. However, some cultural practices are perceived as violations of human rights. This is particularly the case with FGM, which has been consistently and unequivocally condemned in numerous human rights instruments, including the Convention on the Elimination of All Forms of Discrimination against Women (1979), and the Declaration on the Elimination of Violence against Women (1993).

Despite frequent international condemnations and increasing national legislation to criminalize FGM, the practice persists, with some of its defenders claiming that such condemnations and forms of action amount to cultural intolerance.

Prevalence of Female Genital Mutilation

Estimated prevalence of female genital mutilation in girls and women 15–49 years
2009 or latest available data

- almost universal: *90% or more*
- common practice: *50% – 90%*
- less common practice: *5% – 50%*
- minor incidence: *less than 5%, often practised only among small groups or communities*
- imported incidence: *practised within some immigrant groups, where known*
- other countries

What the law says...

Violence against women shall be understood to encompass, but not be limited to, the following: Physical, sexual and psychological violence occurring in the family, including battering, sexual abuse of female children in the household, dowry-related violence, marital rape, female genital mutilation and other traditional practices harmful to women, non-spousal violence and violence related to exploitation.

UN Declaration on the Elimination of Violence against Women, 1993, Article 2

FGM Facts

- FGM includes procedures that intentionally alter or injure female genital organs for non-medical reasons.
- It is mostly carried out between infancy and age 15 years.
- The procedure has no health benefits.
- Procedures can cause severe bleeding and problems urinating.
- Later, it can lead to childbirth complications and newborn deaths.

Legal status of FGM

as of 2008

- banned by law
- banned in some states
- no existing legislation against FGM in countries where it is known to be common practice
- other countries

Several governments, including Australia, Canada, France, Sweden and the USA, have established the legal precedent of giving asylum to women and girls who are fleeing countries where FGM is widely practised.

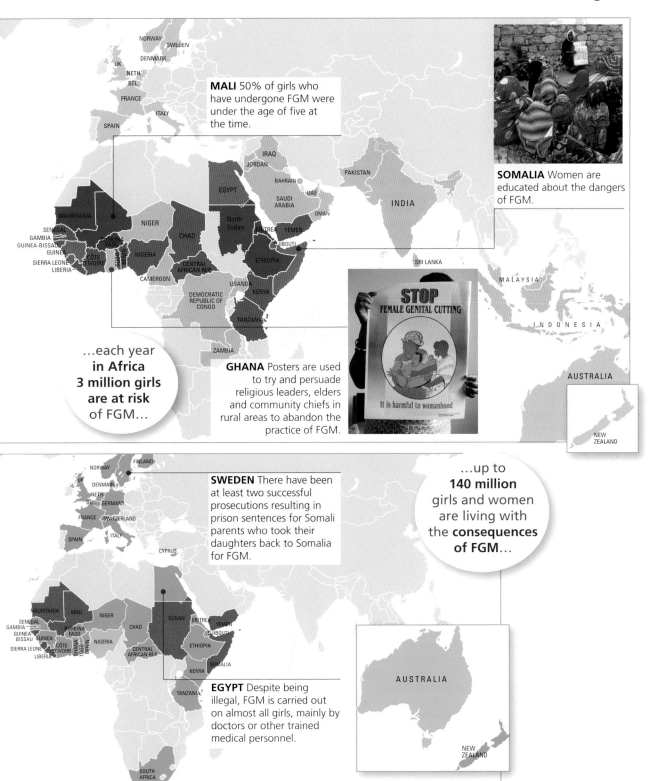

MALI 50% of girls who have undergone FGM were under the age of five at the time.

SOMALIA Women are educated about the dangers of FGM.

...each year **in Africa 3 million girls are at risk** of FGM...

GHANA Posters are used to try and persuade religious leaders, elders and community chiefs in rural areas to abandon the practice of FGM.

STOP FEMALE GENITAL CUTTING
It is harmful to womanhood

SWEDEN There have been at least two successful prosecutions resulting in prison sentences for Somali parents who took their daughters back to Somalia for FGM.

...up to **140 million** girls and women are living with the **consequences of FGM**...

EGYPT Despite being illegal, FGM is carried out on almost all girls, mainly by doctors or other trained medical personnel.

Sex Slavery

The human rights doctrine is founded on the notion that each human being possesses inherent value, and that no human being should be reduced to the status of a mere commodity.

The global sex-trafficking of women and young girls, which perpetuates the centuries-old slave trade, is not only a human rights violation in itself, but its victims face conditions that severely restrict many other human rights as well – the rights to free movement, freedom from cruel and degrading treatment and even the right to life. Since those trafficked across national borders invariably enter the country illegally and thus have no citizenship status, they are also deprived of access to health services and other social benefits.

The global sex-trafficking trade represents another symptom of a general global inequality, with the vast majority of source countries being among the poorer nations of the world, whilst the destination countries are invariably the wealthier nations.

Despite the fact that nearly all the world's governments have signed both CEDAW, 1979, and the Convention on the Rights of the Child, 1989, thereby pledging to ensure legal protection to women and children from traffickers, the global sex-trafficking trade continues to violate the human rights of many millions of women and girls around the globe.

What the law says...

States Parties shall take all appropriate measures, including legislation, to suppress all forms of traffic in women and exploitation of prostitution of women.

Convention on the Elimination of All Forms of Discrimination against Women, 1979 (CEDAW), Article 6

Trafficking

Assessment by US State Department of country compliance with Trafficking Victims Protection Act (TVPA) and selected major trafficking routes
2009

- fully complies with minimum standards established by TVPA
- does not fully comply but is making significant efforts to do so
- does not fully comply, is making significant efforts but there is still evidence of severe forms of trafficking
- does not fully comply
- selected trafficking flows

Prosecution

Regional prosecutions and convictions for sex trafficking
2008

- prosecution
- convictions

Region	Prosecution	Convictions
Africa	109	90
Near East	120	26
The Americas & Caribbean	448	161
South & Central Asia	644	342
East Asia & Pacific	1,803	643
Europe	2,808	1,721

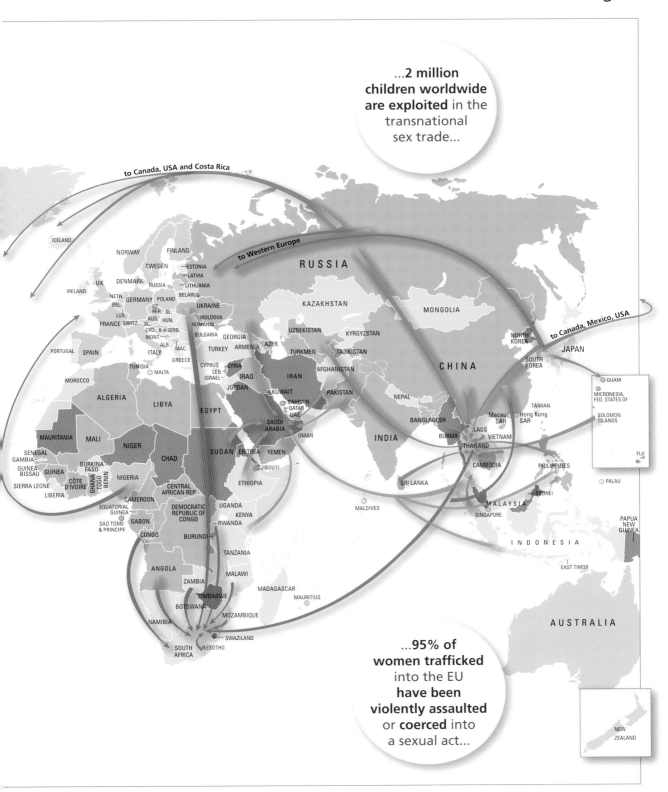

...**2 million children worldwide are exploited** in the transnational sex trade...

to Canada, USA and Costa Rica

to Western Europe

to Canada, Mexico, USA

ICELAND

NORWAY   FINLAND

SWEDEN   ESTONIA
          LATVIA
RUSSIA   LITHUANIA
BELARUS

RUSSIA

UK   DENMARK
IRELAND
NETH.   GERMANY POLAND
BEL.
LUX.   AUS. HUN.   UKRAINE
FRANCE SWITZ. SL.
CRO. B-H SERB.
MONT.   BULGARIA   GEORGIA
ALB.   MAC.
PORTUGAL SPAIN ITALY GREECE   TURKEY ARMENIA
                CYPRUS   AZER.
                LEB. SYRIA
                ISRAEL IRAQ   IRAN
TUNISIA MALTA   JORDAN
MOROCCO   KUWAIT
                  BAHRAIN
ALGERIA LIBYA   QATAR
                  UAE
          EGYPT   SAUDI
                  ARABIA   OMAN
MAURITANIA MALI NIGER
                  SUDAN ERITREA YEMEN
SENEGAL   CHAD   DJIBOUTI
GAMBIA
GUINEA GUINEA BURKINA NIGERIA
BISSAU   FASO
SIERRA LEONE CÔTE GHANA CENTRAL ETHIOPIA
LIBERIA   D'IVOIRE TOGO AFRICAN REP.
          BENIN
          CAMEROON
EQUATORIAL   DEMOCRATIC UGANDA
GUINEA   REPUBLIC OF KENYA
SAO TOME GABON   CONGO   RWANDA
& PRINCIPE CONGO BURUNDI
                  TANZANIA

KAZAKHSTAN

UZBEKISTAN KYRGYZSTAN

TURKMEN. TAJIKISTAN

AFGHANISTAN

PAKISTAN

NEPAL

INDIA   BANGLADESH

SRI LANKA

MALDIVES

MONGOLIA

CHINA

NORTH
KOREA
          JAPAN
SOUTH
KOREA

TAIWAN

Macau Hong Kong
SAR   SAR

LAOS
BURMA VIETNAM
THAILAND

CAMBODIA PHILIPPINES

MALAYSIA

BRUNEI

SINGAPORE

INDONESIA

EAST TIMOR

GUAM

MICRONESIA,
FED. STATES OF

SOLOMON
ISLANDS

FIJI

PALAU

PAPUA
NEW
GUINEA

AUSTRALIA

ANGOLA

ZAMBIA   MALAWI
ZIMBABWE   MADAGASCAR
BOTSWANA   MAURITIUS
          MOZAMBIQUE
NAMIBIA
          SWAZILAND
SOUTH LESOTHO
AFRICA

...**95%** of **women trafficked** into the EU **have been violently assaulted** or **coerced** into a sexual act...

NEW
ZEALAND

Part 7

Children's Rights

Human rights exist in order to protect the most vulnerable members of the global human community. One of the most vulnerable groups is children, who are compelled to live in a world not of their own making.

Some human rights violations affect only children, such as the denial of a right to education or the use of child soldiers in armed conflicts. Other violations affect everybody, but have the greatest impact upon children. These include the denial of a right to health and to be free from the effects of absolute poverty.

Children's human rights have been enshrined within the 1989 Convention on the Rights of the Child, but despite this their abuse and violation remain depressingly widespread and far-reaching. An estimated 9 million children die every year before they reach the age of five. A child dies from hunger every six seconds. The principal causes are absolute poverty, destitution and lack of basic healthcare and sanitation.

Terrible though such statistics are, they mark only the tip of the iceberg of the violation of children's human rights. Many children who survive beyond the age of five are exposed to appalling conditions. Around 190 million children aged between 5 and 14 are employed in some form of economic activity, many of them exposed to dangerous and demeaning conditions and long working days. In many cases these conditions have long-standing effects on children's health, development and well-being.

Around 100 million children are not attending any form of schooling. There are a multitude of reasons and explanations for this denial of their human rights. There may be no available schools for children to attend, or the schools that do exist are simply too distant for some children to reach them. In some cases, girls will be prevented from attending school by their families on the grounds that only the most basic education is needed to perform the traditional roles allocated to them. Last, but not least, there are an estimated 300,000 child soldiers actively involved in wars and armed conflict in the world today. While many children die before ever having had an opportunity to become adults, others are effectively denied the opportunity of ever enjoying a childhood.

MADAGASCAR: A young brick-carrier with a heavy load.

Child Labour

Over 190 million children aged between 5 and 14 years are estimated to be employed in some form of economic activity.

The vast majority work in the agricultural sector, and child labour is generally much higher in rural areas than in urban ones. Often, children will be working not for wages but simply to help the family survive: collecting water, keeping watch over precious livestock, and producing and preparing food.

International human rights law does not specifically forbid children from working, but aims to protect them from employment that adversely affects their human rights. An estimated 126 million children are involved in some form of hazardous labour, such as working in mines, factories and construction projects, and operating machinery, where they run the risk of chronic illness, blindness, of losing their limbs or even their life.

Family poverty is the fundamental reason why many children are compelled to earn money, but as well as damaging children's health and physical development, work adversely affects their social development. They are usually unable to attend school and are therefore denied the opportunity to break out of the grip of the poverty to which they are otherwise condemned.

While the number of working children appears to be gradually declining, the continuing extent to which many industries employ large numbers of children under terms and conditions that are significantly worse than those of their adult counterparts constitutes harmful exploitation of those caught up in this part of the global economic system.

What the law says...

States Parties recognize the right of the child to be protected from economic exploitation and from performing any work that is likely to be hazardous or to interfere with the child's education, or to be harmful to the child's health or physical, mental, spiritual, moral or social development.

Convention on the Rights of the Child, 1989, Article 32

...over **101 million children** worldwide are estimated to be **not attending school**...

Bonded Labour
Producing carpets for export is an important aspect of many South Asian economies. In Pakistan, as many as 50 percent of carpet weavers are children under the age of 14. Many work 12 hours a day or more for wages up to one-third less than those received by their adult counterparts. Under the so-called "Peshgi system", widespread in the Pakistan carpet industry, many of the children are effectively bonded labourers. The system provides a cash advance for very poor families in return for which their children become carpet weavers. Children are unable to leave or complain about their working conditions until the money has been repaid, which typically takes many years.

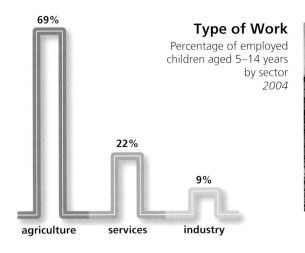

69%

22%

9%

agriculture services industry

Type of Work
Percentage of employed
children aged 5–14 years
by sector
2004

EGYPT Children as young
as five years of age often
work all day in the fields
for a paltry wage.

Working Children
Regional distribution of
economically active children
aged 5–14 years
2004

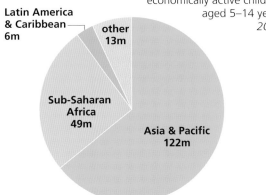

Latin America
& Caribbean
6m

other
13m

Sub-Saharan
Africa
49m

Asia & Pacific
122m

Total: 190 million

UGANDA Instead of
attending school, children
living near Lake Katwe
earn money for their
families by carrying basins
of salt.

Declining Incidence
Economically active children
aged 5–14 years
as percentage of
regional total
2000 & 2004

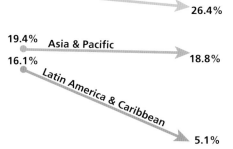

28.8% Sub-Saharan Africa
26.4%

19.4% Asia & Pacific
18.8%

16.1%
Latin America & Caribbean
5.1%

BANGLADESH Young
children are employed to
sort fish for drying.

Child Soldiers

There are an estimated 300,000 soldiers under the age of 18, waging war across the world.

Some children wield assault rifles, machetes, or rocket-propelled grenades on the front lines. Others are used in "combat support" roles, as messengers, spies, cooks, mine-clearers, porters and sexual slaves. It is not uncommon for them to participate in killing and raping.

Child soldiers in the militias of warlords, insurgency groups and rebel forces tend to be between the ages of 14 and 17, but some as young as seven have been recorded. Boys and girls are "recruited" through a variety of methods. Sometimes parents offer their children as a means of combating poverty, or children may offer to fight in the hope of protecting themselves and their families from warring parties, or because they identify with a particular warring cause. In many cases, however, children are simply kidnapped by forces as they pass through villages and communities. The ex-President of Liberia, Charles Taylor, was tried in the International Court of Human Rights in The Hague for, among other atrocities, recruiting child soldiers.

The Optional Protocol on the involvement of children in armed conflict entered into force in 2002, and by 2009 had been ratified by 128 countries. It prohibits the compulsory recruitment, or deployment in hostilities, of soldiers under the age of 18. The USA and UK military forces recruit from the age of 17 years, but since signing the Optional Protocol have taken steps to prevent under-18s being sent to conflict zones. In 2009, Rifleman William Aldridge was deployed by the British army to Afghanistan three days after his 18th birthday, and was killed 45 days later.

What the law says...

States Parties shall take all feasible measures to ensure that members of their armed forces who have not attained the age of 18 years do not take a direct part in hostilities [and] that persons who have not attained the age of 18 years are not compulsorily recruited into their armed forces.

Optional Protocol (2000) to the Convention on the Rights of the Child (1989), Articles 1 & 2

Ex-Child Soldiers Speak

"It disturbs me so much that I inflicted death on other people. When I go home I must do some traditional rites ... and cleanse myself. I still dream about the boy from my village that I killed. ... He is talking to me, saying I killed him for nothing, and I am crying."

A 16-year-old girl after demobilization from an armed group

"Being new, I couldn't perform the very difficult exercises properly and so I was beaten every morning. Two of my friends died because of the beatings. The soldiers buried them in the latrines. I am still thinking of them."

Former child soldier

Children of Violence

Countries where under-18s were recruited or used in hostilities
2004–07

COLOMBIA Children are used by armed opposition groups as combatants and mine layers. If captured, they may be interrogated by government forces. Others, like this 13-year-old, who has reputedly killed five people, are also used as hired assassins in disputes between paramilitary groups and drug dealers.

ISRAEL and PALESTINIAN TERRITORIES Children are involved on both sides. Israeli children have been used by extreme settler movements in violent activities. The Israeli military are alleged to have used Palestinian children as shields, and have arrested and interrogated thousands of teenagers, such as 14-year-old Abdel Al-Rahman Ahmadtite, usually for throwing stones.

NEPAL During the 10-year Maoists' People's War against the Nepalese monarchy, children were enlisted on both sides, but following the peace agreement of 2006 steps were taken to rescue and rehabilitate them, with the help of UN agencies.

IRAQ
AFGHANISTAN
INDIA
SUDAN
CÔTE D'IVOIRE
SRI LANKA
THAILAND
PHILIPPINES
UGANDA   SOMALIA
BURUNDI
INDONESIA

CHAD Children have been recruited by the government from refugee camps along its eastern border for use as border guards. Despite an agreement to demobilize child soldiers, up to 10,000 were estimated to remain in government and militia forces in 2007.

CENTRAL AFRICAN REPUBLIC Child soldiers were used by both sides in a dispute that broke out between two armed groups in 2005, including this child, sporting an AC Milan football shirt.

DEMOCRATIC REPUBLIC OF THE CONGO At least 7,000 child soldiers are involved in the conflicts that continue to erupt in the east of the country. Most have horrific accounts of their brutal and brutalizing training.

BURMA Thousands of children are used as soldiers in the ongoing disputes between the government and ethnic groups fighting for independence. These children are part of the Karenni Army guerrillas.

Education

Education is a core right and the basis for obtaining a wide range of other human rights.

Children have a fundamental right to primary education. Nearly all the countries of the world have ratified the Convention on the Rights of the Child, thereby making a commitment to provide free, universal primary education, and to develop a range of secondary-level facilities.

The industrialized nations lead the way in the provision of formal primary and secondary schooling, but since the early 1990s significant progress has been made in many parts of the developing world in achieving higher levels of school enrolment, and in reducing the long-standing disparity in the enrolment of boys and girls.

A number of factors are crucial in increasing school enrolment: higher government expenditure on education, higher household incomes, higher female literacy rates, a greater proportion of women in paid employment, and a greater proportion of the population living in urban areas, where access to schools is easier.

Many challenges remain. An increase in school enrolment does not necessarily mean that children are present in the classroom on a regular basis, and non-attendance remains high in many parts of the developing world. Nor do enrolment rates measure the quality of education, which has much to do with the facilities provided and the number of pupils in a class. A shortage of trained teachers remains a serious obstacle to the provision of adequate education in many countries.

What the law says...

States Parties recognize the right of the child to education, and with a view to achieving this right progressively and on the basis of equal opportunity, they shall, in particular

(a) Make primary education compulsory and available free to all;

(b) Encourage the development of different forms of secondary education, including general and vocational education, make them available and accessible to every child...

UN Convention on the Rights of the Child, 1989, Article 28

Primary Enrolment

Percentage of children of primary-school age enrolled *latest available 2000–07*

- 90% or more
- 70% – 89%
- 50% – 69%
- 30% – 49%
- no data

Enrolment of girls compared with that of boys:

10 – 27 percentage points lower

NICARAGUA State spending on education doubled between 1999 and 2003

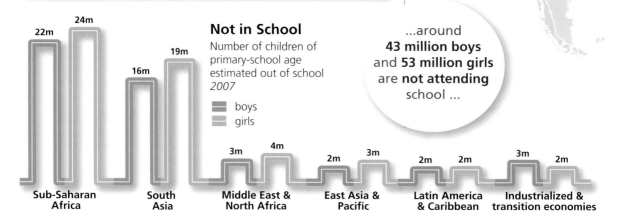

Not in School

Number of children of primary-school age estimated out of school *2007*

- boys
- girls

...around **43 million boys** and **53 million girls** are **not attending** school ...

22m · 24m · 16m · 19m — Sub-Saharan Africa · South Asia
3m · 4m — Middle East & North Africa
2m · 3m — East Asia & Pacific
2m · 2m — Latin America & Caribbean
3m · 2m — Industrialized & transition economies

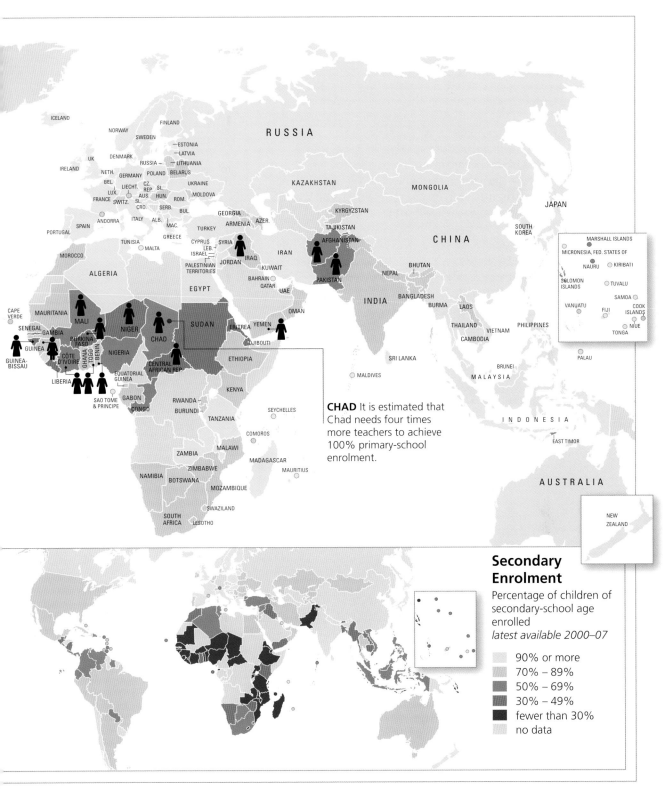

ICELAND
NORWAY
FINLAND
SWEDEN
ESTONIA
LATVIA
UK DENMARK RUSSIA LITHUANIA
IRELAND NETH. GERMANY POLAND BELARUS
BEL LIECHT. CZ. SL. UKRAINE
LUX. AUS. HUN. MOLDOVA
FRANCE SWITZ. SL. ROM.
CRO. SERB. BUL.
ANDORRA ITALY ALB. MAC. GEORGIA
PORTUGAL SPAIN GREECE ARMENIA AZER.
TUNISIA MALTA CYPRUS TURKEY
MOROCCO ISRAEL SYRIA
PALESTINIAN JORDAN IRAQ
TERRITORIES BAHRAIN
QATAR
ALGERIA EGYPT UAE
CAPE MAURITANIA
VERDE
SENEGAL MALI NIGER SUDAN ERITREA YEMEN
GAMBIA BURKINA CHAD OMAN
GUINEA FASO
GUINEA- CÔTE NIGERIA DJIBOUTI
BISSAU D'IVOIRE GHANA CENTRAL ETHIOPIA
TOGO AFRICAN REP.
LIBERIA BENIN
SAO TOME GABON KENYA
& PRINCIPE CONGO RWANDA
BURUNDI TANZANIA SEYCHELLES
COMOROS
ZAMBIA MALAWI
ZIMBABWE MADAGASCAR
NAMIBIA MAURITIUS
BOTSWANA
MOZAMBIQUE
SWAZILAND
SOUTH LESOTHO
AFRICA

RUSSIA
KAZAKHSTAN MONGOLIA JAPAN
KYRGYZSTAN SOUTH
TAJIKISTAN KOREA
AFGHANISTAN CHINA
PAKISTAN BHUTAN
NEPAL
INDIA BANGLADESH
BURMA LAOS
THAILAND VIETNAM
CAMBODIA PHILIPPINES
SRI LANKA BRUNEI
MALDIVES MALAYSIA
INDONESIA
EAST TIMOR
AUSTRALIA

MARSHALL ISLANDS
MICRONESIA, FED. STATES OF
NAURU KIRIBATI
SOLOMON TUVALU
ISLANDS SAMOA
VANUATU FIJI COOK
ISLANDS
NIUE
TONGA
PALAU

NEW
ZEALAND

CHAD It is estimated that Chad needs four times more teachers to achieve 100% primary-school enrolment.

Secondary Enrolment

Percentage of children of secondary-school age enrolled
latest available 2000–07

- 90% or more
- 70% – 89%
- 50% – 69%
- 30% – 49%
- fewer than 30%
- no data

Child Mortality & Health

Of all of the human rights children possess, their rights to life and to the enjoyment of health are most at threat around the globe.

The risk of a child dying in much of the developed world is very low, while in the developing world it is an all-too-frequent occurrence. In 2007, an estimated 9 million children died before they reached the age of five. Of these, over 3 million died within the first month of life.

The likelihood of such a personal catastrophe is affected by a number of factors, many of which are preventable. They include high levels of HIV/AIDS, lack of immunization, lack of trained health professionals, lack of access to clean water and sanitation, lack of insecticides and mosquito nets, and even exposure to armed conflict. They also include level of household income, with wide discrepancies existing between child deaths among the richest and poorest within any country.

Children in many parts of the developing world also suffer from poor health and lack an adequately nutritious diet. In 2007, it was estimated that 112 million under-fives were underweight. It is encouraging that this represents a 7-percent decrease on the 1990 figures, but undernourishment remains a significant factor in over one-third of all deaths of children in this age group.

Child Deaths

Under-five mortality rate per 1,000 live births
2007

- 150 – 262
- 100 – 149
- 50 – 99
- 10 – 49
- fewer than 10
- no data

...every **6 seconds** a child **dies** **of hunger**...

Underweight Children

Percentage of under-fives underweight for age
latest available 2000–07
countries with highest incidence

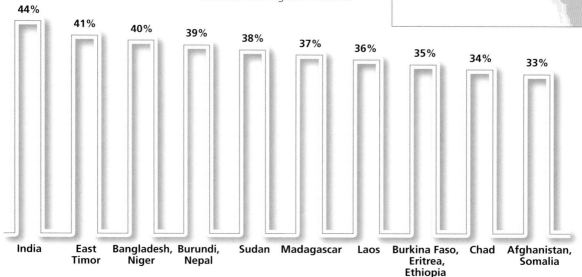

44%	41%	40%	39%	38%	37%	36%	35%	34%	33%
India	East Timor	Bangladesh, Niger	Burundi, Nepal	Sudan	Madagascar	Laos	Burkina Faso, Eritrea, Ethiopia	Chad	Afghanistan, Somalia

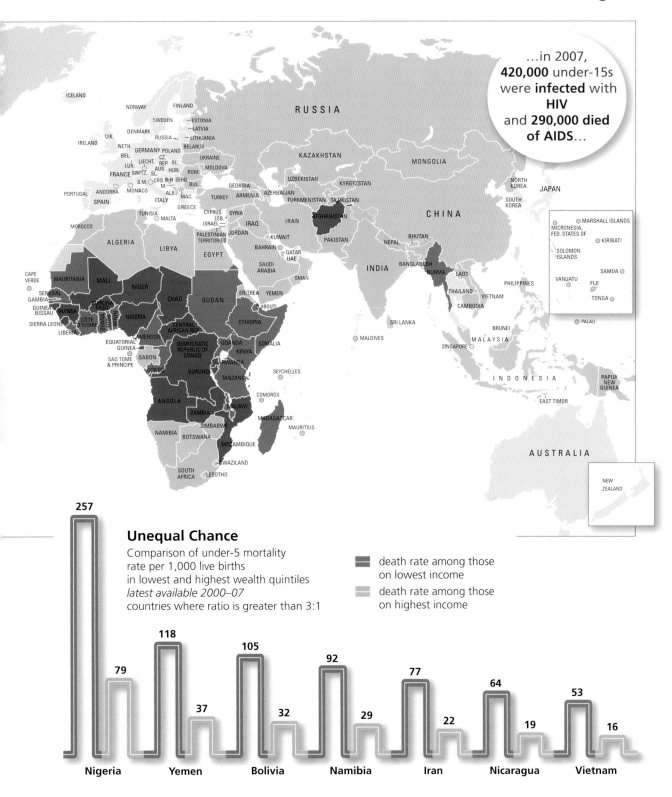

...in 2007, **420,000** under-15s were **infected** with **HIV** and **290,000 died of AIDS**...

Unequal Chance
Comparison of under-5 mortality rate per 1,000 live births in lowest and highest wealth quintiles *latest available 2000–07* countries where ratio is greater than 3:1

death rate among those on lowest income

death rate among those on highest income

257 | 79 | Nigeria
118 | 37 | Yemen
105 | 32 | Bolivia
92 | 29 | Namibia
77 | 22 | Iran
64 | 19 | Nicaragua
53 | 16 | Vietnam

Part 8

COUNTRY PROFILES & WORLD DATA

All nation-states everywhere violate human rights to some degree. Some states do so systematically and extensively; other states do so only occasionally. The struggle for human rights remains a truly global challenge and phenomenon.

This part of the atlas contains brief summary snap-shot accounts of the persisting human rights issues in the vast majority of the world's nation-states – from the most powerful and affluent to the most vulnerable and impoverished. The data has been compiled from a range of different sources.

Cataloguing human rights abuses is no simple task, and necessarily confronts a number of obstacles, foremost of which is the hostility of violators of human rights to having the full extent of their abuses accurately documented. State secrecy, inadequate freedom of information legislation and the lack of extensive statistical data-gathering all confront human rights defenders' attempts to gain a clear picture of the breadth and depth of human rights violations.

Despite these obstacles, reliable indications of headline human rights violations are available and provide the basis for the profiles presented here. As has often been said, knowledge is power and, in this instance, it provides a basis by which the human rights abuses and violations of the powerful may be accurately discerned and challenged.

PAPUA NEW GUINEA: A tally officer keeping count in the 2007 election.

Country Profiles

The following are summaries of the main human rights issues in selected countries.

AFGHANISTAN The human rights situation remains very poor. Ongoing armed conflict between NATO forces and Taliban militia has led to a lack of personal security, disruption of food and water supplies and the destruction of houses. Although elections have been held, the country has been consistently criticized for restrictions on freedom of expression. While the conditions of women have improved from the low point of Taliban rule, women in Afghanistan are still subject to restrictions on many of their human rights. Adult life-expectancy is currently 43 years. Afghanistan retains the death penalty.

ALBANIA Although the country is seeking membership of the European Union, its human rights record raises concerns in some areas. The rights of women remain problematic, with high levels of domestic violence and an established trade in trafficked women. It has been criticized for the poor conditions experienced by those held in its prisons, and allegations of torture and ill-treatment have been made against security and police forces.

ALGERIA The country is experiencing widespread political violence, resulting in significant loss of life. In addition, it has been condemned for restrictions on freedom of expression, continuing violence and discrimination against women, and the impunity enjoyed by state officials who have killed, tortured and harmed Algerian citizens. The security forces have also been condemned for secretly and arbitrarily detaining people suspected of involvement in opposition or terrorist organizations.

ANGOLA Adult life-expectancy in Angola is just 42 years. Widespread poverty and disease continues to wreak havoc on the living conditions of many Angolans. In addition, the authorities have been criticized for human rights abuses in areas such as forced evictions, systematic abuses perpetrated by security and police officials, very poor prison conditions, restrictions on freedom of expression and discrimination against women.

ARGENTINA Although the country's human rights record has improved significantly since the rule of the military juntas in the 1970s and 80s, Argentina has been criticized for continuing discrimination against an ever-diminishing population of indigenous people. The living conditions of people held in its prisons have also attracted consistent criticism.

ARMENIA Border disputes with neighbouring Azerbaijan continue to affect security concerns in Armenia. More specifically, restrictions on freedom of expression have intensified, as have allegations of attempts to restrict political opposition movements. Journalists and media outlets have also reported intimidation and harassment by state officials.

AUSTRALIA Many citizens enjoy some of the best public services in the world. The adult life expectancy is 81 years, and Australia is considered one of the most developed nations on earth. Despite this, it has been consistently condemned for its long-standing discrimination against indigenous peoples. Its treatment of refugees and asylum seekers has also attracted significant criticism.

AUSTRIA Although a member of the EU and a signatory of the European Convention on Human Rights, Austria has been criticized for its treatment of refugees and asylum-seekers. Concerns have also been raised over the alleged ill-treatment of detainees in police custody.

AZERBAIJAN The country has been consistently criticized for restrictions upon freedom of expression and assembly, which tend to be further tightened in the run-up to, and during, elections. Journalists have also complained about harassment and intimidation. Allegations of torture in police custody have also been made. The conditions of internally displaced people from the conflict in Nagorno-Karabakh in the 1990s remain poor.

BAHAMAS The country has been criticized for its human rights record in two principal respects: it has the highest incidence of reported rapes in the world, and the government strongly supports retention of the death penalty.

BAHRAIN The country's human rights record has been criticized in a number of areas, including restrictions on freedom of expression, violations of human rights perpetrated by security and police officials under the auspices of a counter-terrorism policy, continuing practice of arbitrary arrest and detention, and its retention of the death penalty.

BANGLADESH A state of emergency was imposed in 2008 in response to widespread political violence, and has led to restrictions on freedom of assembly, speech and association. In addition, allegations of torture and ill-treatment by security and police officials are widespread. A principal human rights concern is the use of arbitrary arrest and detention, with a reported 440,000 people being arbitrarily detained in 2008. In addition, violence against women remains widespread. Bangladesh executed over 90 convicted people in 2008.

BELARUS In December 2008, Belarus was subject to a UN resolution condemning its human rights record. Opposition groups face persistent harassment and imprisonment, there are extensive restrictions on freedom of assembly and expression, various religious communities continue to face widespread government-backed discrimination, and women continue to suffer discrimination, high rates of domestic violence and trafficking.

BELGIUM The country has been criticized for its treatment of migrants, refugees and asylum-seekers.

BENIN Adult life-expectancy is 55 years. The country has been criticized for excessive use of force by some of its police officials and for poor prison conditions.

BOLIVIA The country has the highest proportion of indigenous people in South America, and elected the first indigenous President in 2006. President Morales has pursued a programme of constitutional change which has divided Bolivia and been accompanied by protests and riots. Bolivia has also been criticized for restrictions on freedom of expression and attacks against journalists.

BOSNIA & HERZEGOVINA The country has been trying to overcome the effects of the Balkan wars in the 1990s. The International Criminal Tribunal for the Former Yugoslavia has been attempting to bring to justice numerous people accused of war crimes and crimes against humanity, with some limited success. More generally, there have been allegations of abuse and ill-treatment by police and prison detainees. Some minorities continue to face discrimination, and the return of refugees displaced by the war has been slow.

BRAZIL Despite an adult life expectancy of 72 years, and relatively high gross domestic income, there are millions of people in Brazil suffering the typical effects of abject poverty. Police operations in many marginalized urban communities have resulted in thousands of deaths. Forced labour and exploitative working conditions continue to affect many. Indigenous peoples continue to suffer the effects of systemic neglect and discrimination.

BULGARIA One of the most recent members of the EU, it has been criticized for its treatment of Roma and minority Macedonian communities. Many asylum-seekers and refugees face long-term detention in poor conditions.

BURMA The military dictatorship continues to defy international pressure and criticism of its poor human rights record. Suppression of any dissent and political protest, combined with far-reaching constraints on freedom of expression and association, serve to quell political opposition. The persecution and killing of ethnic minorities continues. Forced labour is widespread and systematic. There are large numbers of arbitrary detentions, more than 1,000 political prisoners, and numerous cases of disappearances. Prison conditions are generally appalling. Reports of torture are frequently made and there are numerous reported deaths in custody.

BURUNDI Adult life-expectancy is 49 years. Burundi has been condemned on a number of human rights grounds including very poor conditions in detention, high levels of arbitrary arrest and detention, allegations of torture, restrictions on freedom of expression, and widespread sexual violence.

CAMBODIA Claims to land and forced evictions are major human rights concerns. Continuing land disputes and land-grabs place an estimated 150,000 people at risk of losing their homes. Refugees and asylum-seekers face discrimination, and various human rights organizations have been subject to harassment and closure.

CAMEROON Adult life-expectancy is 50 years. Cameroon has been criticized for intimidation of journalists, and for restricting freedom of expression. Sexual minorities face state discrimination and a number of people have been detained for practising homosexuality. Prison conditions are poor, with reports of prisoners being killed in detention.

CANADA Adult life-expectancy is one of the highest in the world at 80 years. Canada has been consistently criticized for discrimination against indigenous people, who face persistent threats to their land, customs and culture.

CENTRAL AFRICAN REPUBLIC This is one of the poorest countries in the world, and has a life-expectancy of 44 years. In addition to the effects of crippling poverty, one of the principal human rights concerns is the lack of security, with widespread violence, destruction of houses and rape practised by armed gangs and government forces alike. In 2008, tens of thousands fled CAR and sought refugee status in neighbouring countries.

CHAD The effects of long-standing civil war and armed conflict remain the principal human rights concern. In September 2008, the UN Security Council resolved to deploy a peacekeeping force in eastern Chad in an attempt to stem the death-toll. Children are vulnerable to abduction and being trafficked, or deployed as child soldiers in various militia groups. Sexual violence is widespread and journalists face systematic intimidation and restrictions. Chad also houses almost 400,000 refugees from Darfur and the Central African Republic.

CHILE Its human rights record has improved since Pinochet's rule ended in 1990, but Chile is criticized for discriminating against its indigenous people.

CHINA The country with the world's largest population has a human rights record that has attracted long-standing and wide-ranging criticism. The main issues are the lack of democratic rights, the widespread use of arbitrary detention, extensive use of the death penalty, discrimination against religious minorities, censorship and restrictions on freedom of expression and speech, the use of torture, discrimination against women and the continuing denial of autonomy to Tibet.

COLOMBIA The ongoing effects of a 40-year conflict between government and militia groups have greatly affected the human rights of Colombians caught up in the conflict, many of whom have become internally displaced. In addition, widespread poverty militates against the establishment of basic economic and social rights. Colombia has also been criticized for restrictions on trade union membership and activities.

CONGO, DEMOCRATIC REPUBLIC OF THE Adult life-expectancy is a mere 46 years. In part, this is a consequence of crippling poverty and long-standing armed conflict and civil war. The DRC has also been heavily condemned for unlawful killings, arbitrary detention and torture, all perpetrated by security officials. There are many child soldiers caught up in the conflicts, 1.4 million internally displaced persons, and a further 320,000 living as refugees in neighbouring countries.

CONGO The country is emerging out of a period of sustained civil and armed conflict. Congo is rich in mineral wealth, particularly diamonds. However, much of this wealth is lost to ordinary Congolese through smuggling and corruption. Congo has been criticized for discrimination against its native Pygmy population, widespread use of arbitrary detention and very poor prison conditions.

CÔTE D'IVOIRE AAdult life-expectancy is 47 years. A UN peacekeeping force remains deployed in an attempt to secure peace between government and militia forces. There are allegations of human rights violations by both sides. Violence against women is widespread, extending to allegations of sexual abuse perpetrated by UN peacekeepers.

CROATIA During Croatia's pursuit of EU membership it has been criticized for failing to bring to justice numerous Croatians accused of war crimes during the Balkan war of the 1990s, and for its discriminatory polices towards minorities, including the Roma and Croatian Serbs.

CUBA Despite the country's economic plight, Cubans generally enjoy excellent welfare and healthcare treatment, reflected in the adult life expectancy of 77.7 years. However, Cuba's record on civil and political rights is far from exemplary. Extensive restrictions on freedom of movement, association and assembly continue. There are an estimated 62 political prisoners in Cuban prisons. A number of journalists have faced intimidation and harassment.

CYPRUS, REPUBLIC OF The principal human rights issues concern harassment and ill-treatment of migrants and asylum-seekers. Some are held in administrative detention for long periods of time without access to lawyers; others report having been beaten by police officers whilst in detention.

CZECH REPUBLIC Discrimination against minorities, particularly Roma people, remains one of the main human rights issues. Some Roma women have even been subjected to forced sterilization.

DENMARK The Council of Europe has criticized the way many asylum-seekers are held in poor conditions for long periods prior to their cases being heard. The country's allocation of social welfare benefits, with significantly lower payments being given to people who have not been permanently resident in Denmark for at least seven of the last eight years, has also been questioned.

DJIBOUTI The country's location on the Gulf of Aden explains the presence of relatively large garrisons of French and US troops, and a significant source of income for Djibouti is overseas development aid. There is widespread poverty. Although the political situation is relatively stable, wide-ranging restrictions on freedom of expression and association are in place.

DOMINICAN REPUBLIC Another Caribbean tourist destination, the Dominican Republic has been criticized for its discrimination against Haitians and Dominco-Haitians. Violence against women is widespread, with little or no response from the authorities. People-trafficking in and out of the Republic remains a significant trade. Journalists and some media organizations have also faced intimidation and harassment.

EAST TIMOR One of the world's newest states, it held its first parliamentary elections in 2007. Attempts are ongoing to bring to justice people accused of recent human rights violations. The threat of continuing civil unrest is a principal factor in the continuing high levels of internally displaced persons.

ECUADOR The government has been pursuing a series of constitutional reforms and has established a truth commission to examine the human rights abuses perpetrated during the 1980s. Despite these positive developments, environmental activists have faced systematic intimidation and harassment in their efforts to combat continuing exploitation of the Amazonian region.

EGYPT Sweeping powers have been granted to security and police officials in Egypt. These have been associated with numerous human rights abuses, foremost of which is the estimated 18,000 people being held under administrative detention, with no effective legal redress. Torture is widespread. There are severe restrictions on freedom of assembly and association, with many groups targeted for alleged links to terrorist organizations. Political activists, journalists and bloggers have been imprisoned. Women's rights are systematically violated, with widespread violence and rape resulting in few prosecutions and inadequate preventive measures. Religious minorities face discrimination. UNHCR estimates that up to 3 million migrants, refugees and asylum-seekers, many from Sudan, are living in Egypt.

EL SALVADOR This country's human rights record has improved significantly since the brutal and bloody regimes of the 1980s. Nevertheless, many of the perpetrators of these earlier human rights abuses have gone unpunished. In addition, the 2006 Special Law Against Acts of Terrorism has been criticized for its effects upon the civil liberties of those targeted under this legislation.

EQUATORIAL GUINEA The government has been criticized for restrictions on the freedom of expression and the detention of political activists. Torture has also been reported by some held in police detention. Life-expectancy for the 500,000-strong population is 50 years.

ERITREA The country has a very poor human rights record. Two-thirds of people depend for their survival on international food aid. Opposition political parties are effectively banned, as are many civil society organizations. Many members of religious faiths banned by the government have been subject to harassment and detention, and there are thousands of political prisoners. Torture is reported to be widespread. The justice system is largely non-existent and most detainees have no legal redress and little prospect of a fair trial. There has been no independent or private press in Eritrea since 2001.

ESTONIA The principal human rights issue in Estonia concerns the rights of the country's linguistic minorities, who comprise some 30 percent of the population. Estonian authorities have placed great emphasis upon the official language but have been slow in providing adequate opportunities for non-Estonian speakers to acquire it. This results in restricted access to public services and discrimination by employers. Estonia has also been criticized by the Council of Europe for the inhumane conditions experienced by many prisoners.

ETHIOPIA Despite earlier optimism in some quarters, Ethiopia's human rights record has taken a turn for the worse. Almost a million people face the threat of starvation in its drought-afflicted regions. Armed conflict between the government and militia groups has also reignited, and Ethiopia continues to engage in armed conflict with Eritrea over disputed borders. There has been a marked increase in the number of political prisoners and others targeted for their religious beliefs. Freedom of expression has been

restricted in various ways. There have been reports of torture within detention facilities.

FIJI A military coup in December 2006, and state of emergency until May 2007, has resulted in a continuing increase in human rights violations. Severe restrictions have been placed on freedom of expression and assembly. Those critical of the military regime have been removed and intimidated, and the judiciary has been targeted. There have also been reports of unlawful arrests and detention. Some of those detained have alleged abuse and torture.

FINLAND The country has been criticized for its unfair treatment of asylum-seekers and refugees. Conscientious objectors to military conscription are imprisoned. Domestic violence is widespread and, despite a recommendation from the UN Committee on Social and Economic Rights, the Finnish government has yet to devise a national plan to combat it.

FRANCE The country continues to be criticized for its treatment of migrants, asylum-seekers and refugees, with repeated allegations of their ill-treatment at the hands of the police. The ban on the display of religious clothing or symbols in public buildings attracts criticism from many quarters, especially from the French Muslim community.

GABON An oil-producing African country, Gabon has had only two presidents since it achieved independence from France in 1964. It has remained politically stable, although protests against French interests broke out in 2008 after claims that presidential elections were rigged. There are large disparities in wealth between rich and poor. Gabon's television, radio and newspapers are state-controlled.

GAMBIA The use of arbitrary detention as a means for silencing and oppressing political opposition to the current regime is a particular concern. The charge of treason has also been used against members of former governments and political opponents. Those charged cannot expect a fair trial. There are significant restrictions on freedom of expression, and many journalists have been intimidated and harassed.

Some have even been charged with sedition for their alleged anti-government writings.

GEORGIA The country has experienced significant political upheaval since its independence. Despite the introduction of various constitutional reforms, the current regime has been subject to concerted criticism and street protests. Some of these protests have resulted in violence between protesters and police. Georgia has been criticized for its detention of political opponents and for the conditions in which prisoners are held. Some Georgians have also had their property requisitioned by state authorities with little or no financial compensation. The country's ongoing dispute with Russia over the regions of South Ossetia and Abkhazia resulted in a short but highly destructive war with Russia in August 2008.

GERMANY There has been criticism of the alleged involvement of German special forces and security personnel in the illegal removal of suspects from Afghanistan as part of the so-called "special rendition" programme, orchestrated by the USA. Allegations of the role of German officials in the alleged rendition of several German nationals of Syrian and Lebanese origin have also been subject to parliamentary scrutiny.

GHANA The country has one of the better records for human rights in Africa, having established an effective national human rights commission and a committee for national reconciliation which seeks to compensate the victims of former regimes. Despite these positive developments, violence against women remains widespread, and female genital mutilation remains a relatively common practice.

GREECE There have been consistent criticisms of the country's treatment of asylum-seekers and refugees, many of whom face long detention in poor conditions before having their applications refused. The Roma community continues to face discrimination and persecution. The trafficking of women continues unabated.

GUATEMALA Security remains a key concern for many Guatemalans who experience high levels of crime and violence. Those involved in the human rights abuses and mass killings of former regimes mostly continue to enjoy effective immunity. Human rights defenders face intimidation and physical attacks. Women continue to face high levels of violence, with little protection from the state.

GUINEA Amidst economic crisis and political instability, protesters have been met with extreme police violence, resulting in many hundreds of deaths. Arbitrary detention and torture whilst in custody have been frequently reported. Freedom of expression is subject to wide-ranging restrictions and many journalists have been arbitrarily detained. Newspaper allegations of government corruption have led to criminal sentences being handed down to editors and proprietors.

GUINEA-BISSAU Many of the inhabitants of Guinea-Bissau face some of the worst economic conditions in Africa. Adult life expectancy is 46 years. Freedom of expression has been severely and systematically restricted, and many journalists have been imprisoned. The trafficking of children out of the country is significant and largely unaddressed by the authorities.

HAITI After decades of political turmoil and civil conflict, UN intervention since 2004 has been credited with improvements in the security situation and the establishment of some degree of political stability. Nevertheless, Haiti continues to suffer from many human rights abuses. Violence against women and girls remains widespread. Freedom of expression is limited. The government has failed to adequately investigate past human rights abuses. Children's access to education is severely affected by poverty, with an estimated 500,000 children not attending school.

HONDURAS The police have been consistently criticized for their ill-treatment and abuse of detainees. Numerous human rights defenders have been exposed to violent intimidation; some have even been murdered. Violence against women is widespread and largely unacknowledged by the state.

HUNGARY The principal human rights issue in Hungary remains the discrimination and persecution suffered by the Roma community. Two UN reports have criticized Hungary for its failure to adequately protect the Roma. Hungary has also been criticized for the detention of asylum-seekers and non-nationals.

INDIA Although often referred to as the "largest democracy in the world", and experiencing rapid economic growth, India suffers from many human rights issues. Some of these are caused by the extreme levels of economic inequality and the hundreds of millions of Indians who live in abject poverty. Other violations stem from long-standing religious and cultural practices and customs which discriminate against marginalized communities. Violence against women remains widespread. Excessive use of force and brutality by police officials is commonplace. Allegations of torture and other human rights abuses in the states of Jammu and Kashmir go un-investigated. India's security situation has been severely affected by numerous terrorist attacks. Muslims have been subjected to systematic intimidation, assault and murder in several Indian states.

INDONESIA Torture and the abuse of detainees by security and police officials remain relatively widespread and ignored by state authorities. There has been a steady increase of political prisoners, as authorities target religious groups alleged to have connections with Islamist terrorist organizations. Many human rights defenders have been subject to harassment and intimidation. The security situation in Papua, which has long sought independence, remains unstable. Discrimination and violence against women remains widespread and a thriving sex-trafficking trade exists. Indonesia has one of the highest rates of maternal mortality in the world, which is exacerbated by women's lack of access to sexual education and reproductive health services.

IRAN The country has been rightly condemned for widespread human rights abuses. Opposition movements face severe restrictions and criminal prosecutions, as do many human rights defenders and civil society organizations. There are comprehensive restrictions on freedom of expression.

The rights of women are subject to wide-ranging limitations and violations. Religious minorities are systematically discriminated against and persecuted. Sexual minorities face severe state persecution. Iran has executed hundreds of convicted criminals in recent years; some have even been stoned to death. Torture is reportedly widespread.

IRAQ. Lack of security is one of the greatest human rights issues in post-Saddam Iraq. Sectarian violence continues to blight the lives of many Iraqis. There are over 2 million Iraqi refugees in neighbouring Syria, Jordan and other states who have fled violence and persecution. A further 2.2 million Iraqis have been internally displaced. The US-led Multinational Force has killed many thousands of civilians as part of its operations. It has also detained more than 25,000 Iraqis who have neither been charged nor tried. The death penalty has been used widely, and women continue to suffer from high levels of violence and other forms of discrimination.

IRELAND The conditions in many of Ireland's prisons have attracted criticism. The reproductive rights of women are restricted in accordance with the Catholic Church's policy on abortion and the right to life.

ISRAEL and PALESTINIAN TERRITORIES The living conditions of many of those in the Occupied Palestinian Territories are lamentable. Many face threats to life and livelihood as a consequence of Israeli policies on Gaza and the West Bank. In Gaza, an estimated 1.5 million Palestinians have suffered from the imposition of a blockade. The building by Israel of the so-called defence wall around the West Bank threatens to imprison the Palestinian population, and is in violation of international law. Palestinian populations in Gaza and the West Bank are effectively dependent upon humanitarian aid. Thousands of Palestinians are subject to arbitrary arrest and long periods of detention. Allegations of torture are widespread. Violence has also erupted between Palestinians and the rival Hamas and Fatah movements.

ITALY Roma communities in Italy face wide-ranging discrimination, as do many migrants and asylum-seekers. Italy's response to the so-called "war on terror" included new legislation that provides for the arrest and immediate removal of migrants suspected of involvement with terrorist groups, effectively denying them fair legal hearings. There have been repeated allegations of ill-treatment and abuse against police officials. Prime Minister Berlusconi's extensive media ownership has raised questions of the effective freedom of the press in Italy.

JAMAICA The principal human rights concern in Jamaica is lack of security, apparent in very high rates of murder and violent crime. Allegations of police brutality are on the increase. There also exists widespread discrimination against women and gay men.

JAPAN Legislation has been passed which largely removes legal obstacles to the deportation of foreign nationals considered by state officials to be involved in terrorist activities. The country continues to refuse to make reparations to the victims of its war crimes and atrocities.

JORDAN Many people have been arrested and detained under anti-terror legislation. Special security tribunals effectively deny the possibility of a fair trial. Some of those detained have allegedly been tortured. Violence against women remains widespread and there are numerous reported cases of so-called "honour killings". Freedom of expression has been restricted, as have freedom of assembly and association. Migrant workers face discrimination and lack of employment protection. Jordan houses some 1.9 million Palestinian refugees and 500,000 refugees from Iraq.

KAZAKHSTAN Kazakhstan's rich gas and oil deposits make it one of the most affluent of the former Soviet Republics. The current President and his political party routinely secure very high majorities in presidential and legislative elections, which are just as routinely criticized by international election monitoring teams. Refugees from China, Russia and Uzbekistan face discrimination and ill-treatment. Some have even been forcibly returned in violation of international law. Freedom of expression is subject to various

restrictions, and a number of independent journalists report intimidation and harassment.

KENYA Once considered one of the success stories of post-colonial Africa, Kenya has been ravaged by severe armed conflict and political instability. Systematic outbreaks of violence in response to the disputed election results of 2007 resulted in hundreds being killed, many more injured and thousands being displaced from their communities and villages. There are over 100,000 internally displaced Kenyans. Human rights abuses by police officers go un-investigated. Many Somali refugees were forcibly returned after Kenya closed its border with Somalia in 2008. Violence against women and girls is widespread. Freedom of expression is subject to various forms of limitation.

KOREA, NORTH The country has one of the worst human rights records in the world. Dissent against the present regime is all but impossible, given the extensive restrictions on freedom of expression, speech, assembly and association. Arbitrary detention is widespread, and imprisonment of people suspected of opposition to the regime is routine and extensive. Hundreds of North Koreans forcibly returned by China after attempting to leave Korea have simply "disappeared". National and international media are subject to far-reaching prohibitions and controls. The death penalty is extensively used. There have been reports of parts of the rural population suffering severe malnutrition.

KOREA, SOUTH The election of a new president in February 2008 led to the reversal of various reforms introduced by the previous government. Restrictions on freedom of expression have been tightened. The continuing use of the 1948 National Security Law has resulted in treason charges being laid against journalists for publishing details of the US military presence in South Korea. Popular protests have been met with a violent response from the police. A number of industrial disputes have similarly been met with forceful interventions by state authorities. Migrant workers face discrimination and inadequate employment protection.

KUWAIT The many migrant workers in Kuwait face severe discrimination and abuse. Many are employed as female domestic workers and there are many reports testifying to systematic physical abuse and ill-treatment. Freedom of expression remains problematic with the targeting of various independent media outlets.

KYRGYZSTAN The human rights situation in this former Soviet Republic has deteriorated in recent years. Political instability and disputed elections have accompanied the introduction of further limitations on civil liberties and opposition groups. Torture is reported to be widespread. Many refugees from Uzbekistan have been forcibly returned. Independent journalists have been intimidated and one journalist was murdered in October 2008.

LAOS Ethnic minorities face severe persecution in Laos, with some being forced to seek refuge in the jungle. More widely, freedom of expression and assembly are subject to extensive control and limitation. Prison conditions have been consistently condemned. A WHO report indicates that over half of the rural population of children in Laos suffer from malnutrition.

LATVIA The single largest human rights issue in Latvia is the 400,000 stateless people living there who are still denied citizenship. Most of these were former residents of the Soviet Union who remained in Latvia after independence. In addition, linguistic minorities continue to face discrimination, as do various sexual minorities.

LEBANON Lebanon's human rights situation is dominated by continuing violence and political instability. Israel's invasion of southern Lebanon in 2006 in its war with Hizbollah resulted in the deaths of hundreds of civilians and many more serious injuries. Women face wide-ranging discrimination, as do many Palestinian refugees. Allegations of torture have been increasing.

LIBERIA Adult life expectancy in Liberia is one of the lowest in the world at 45 years. The human rights situation has improved from the low point of the regime of Charles Taylor, who is being tried for crimes against humanity in The Hague. Nevertheless, many problems remain, including deplorable prison conditions, widespread violence against women and approximately 80,000 Liberians who fled to neighbouring countries and have yet to return.

LIBYA The country's human rights record has attracted significant criticism. Freedom of expression is severely restricted. There are no genuinely independent NGOs there, and human rights defenders and dissidents face prosecution and intimidation. Refugees, asylum-seekers and migrants face wide-ranging discrimination. Women continue to face discrimination and inequality.

LITHUANIA The rights of lesbian, gay, bisexual and transgender people have been routinely violated through the banning of various assemblies and demonstrations.

MACEDONIA The country has been criticized by the UN for its treatment of Roma people, who experience widespread discrimination and persecution. Armed clashes between state forces and ethnic Albanians have also occurred. Violence against women is widespread and child trafficking is largely overlooked by the state. There have been allegations of torture and ill-treatment.

MALAWI The prevalence of HIV/AIDS constitutes one of the greatest challenges, and life-expectancy is only 46 years. It is estimated that 1 million children have been orphaned by AIDS deaths. The economic and social rights of Malawians are also severely affected by extensive poverty and under-investment.

MALAYSIA The Internal Security Act has resulted in an increase in arbitrary detention and a wide-ranging state censorship of media organizations, independent journalists and political dissidents. There have been numerous deaths in custody. Restrictions imposed on various religious groups have been condemned, as has discrimination against ethnic Indians. Migrant workers, asylum-seekers and refugees have been subject to mass arrest.

MALI Political stability in Mali continues to be undermined by conflict between government and militia forces in the north. Freedom of expression has been curtailed and the editors of some newspapers critical of the government have been prosecuted.

MALTA The country has been criticized by the Council of Europe for routinely detaining asylum-seekers and migrants in violation of international law.

MAURITANIA Elections in this Islamic republic were held in December 2006, ending a period of military rule. A human rights commission has been established and some progress has been made in the country's human rights record. The two principal human rights concerns are the detention of political prisoners and widespread allegations of torture.

MEXICO The country suffers from a number of human rights issues, including systematic police violence and abuse of detainees, arbitrary detention and unfair trials, lack of security in several states where murder and violent crimes are widespread, restrictions on freedom of expression and harassment of journalists, intimidation and killing of human rights defenders, continuing persecution of indigenous people, and widespread violence against women.

MOLDOVA Despite the establishment of numerous legal reforms, human rights abuses continue in Moldova. Allegations of torture are frequently made by detainees. Women face the widespread threat of violence and abuse. Men, women and children are trafficked out of the country. Restrictions on freedom of expression and the press persist.

MONGOLIA There has been significant progress in establishing parliamentary democracy and the rule of law since the break-up of the Soviet Union. However, allegations of torture are frequent. There is a significant population of street children in the capital city, and extreme poverty elsewhere in the country. Trafficking of women and children is largely ignored by the state authorities.

MONTENEGRO The country has been criticized for failure to bring to justice suspected war criminals from the Balkan war of the 1990s. Allegations of torture persist and are rarely investigated. The Roma people face discrimination. Trafficking of women has not been adequately addressed by the state.

MOROCCO The country is a monarchy without democratic elections. Freedom of expression, assembly and association are severely limited. Criticism of the monarchy is prohibited and carries heavy prison sentences. Freedom of the press is subject to wide-ranging restrictions. Migrants are routinely arrested and expelled. Violence against women is widespread and men have been imprisoned for homosexual activity.

MOZAMBIQUE Adult life expectancy is 43 years. Crippling poverty blights the lives of many. Other human rights abuses include extra-judicial killings and arbitrary arrests and detentions of protesters. Natural disasters are frequent, typically causing large numbers of displaced persons.

NAMIBIA Former president Sam Nujoma has been threatened with prosecution before the International Criminal Court for alleged crimes against humanity. The new president has sought to implement some reforms. Nevertheless, human rights abuses continue in the form of frequent allegations of torture, widespread violence against women and girls and far-reaching restrictions on freedom of expression.

NEPAL Various reforms have been proposed since the country became a democracy in 2008, but little progress has been made in the pursuit of human rights abusers under earlier regimes. Allegations of police brutality continue. There remain thousands of internally displaced persons and more than 100,000 Bhutanese refugees. Journalists have faced intimidation and harassment. Women and girls face discrimination and widespread violence.

NETHERLANDS Some Dutch local authorities have been criticized for failing to adequately implement anti-discrimination and anti-racism policies. The UN has criticized the Netherlands for not fully protecting the rights of migrant women against the effects of discrimination.

NICARAGUA The principal human rights concern in Nicaragua is women's rights. Abortion is prohibited under all circumstances after the passing of legislation in 2006. This has attracted significant domestic and international criticism.

NIGER Armed conflict between government forces and Tuareg groups remains a central human rights concern in Niger. The conflict has resulted in many civilian deaths and numerous reports of extra-judicial killings. Arbitrary detention is frequently reported and there are consistent allegations of torture. Freedom of expression is subject to extensive restrictions.

NIGERIA Despite significant revenue from oil, adult life-expectancy in Nigeria is 47 years. Periodic elections are held, but are typically accompanied by violence. Communities in the oil-rich Niger delta are persecuted and ill-treated. Extra-judicial killings and torture are frequently reported. Journalists face wide-ranging restrictions and intimidation. Violence against women is widespread. Lesbians and gays face persecution and prosecution.

PAKISTAN A poor security situation continues to blight the lives of many in Pakistan. Arbitrary arrests and detentions are widespread. The judicial system includes a tribal council component in which a fair trial is largely denied. So-called "honour killings" have even been authorized by these councils. Violence against women and girls is widespread, as are forced marriages. The executive has been in conflict with the judiciary and many independent judges have been dismissed. Hostage taking and killing by armed groups is an established feature of some regions. Freedom of expression is subject to extensive limitations. Pakistan's involvement in the "war on terror" has resulted in many hundreds of enforced disappearances. Religious minorities are systematically discriminated against.

PALESTINIAN TERRITORIES *see* **ISRAEL and PALESTINIAN TERRITORIES**

PAPUA NEW GUINEA Civil society has become increasingly fractious and liable to conflict. Personal security is a key human rights issue, with high levels of violent crime and a largely uncontrolled proliferation of small arms smuggled into the country. Violence against women is widespread and largely ignored by the authorities.

PARAGUAY Indigenous peoples bear the brunt of poverty in Paraguay and are subject to wide-ranging forms of discrimination. Peasants have also faced enforced evictions from their land and have alleged ill-treatment by the police.

PERU The country continues to emerge from decades of armed conflict. Significant progress has been made in attempts to bring perpetrators of earlier human rights abuses to justice. The mining industry faces opposition from environmentalists and indigenous peoples, who frequently allege intimidation and ill-treatment as a response to their opposition.

PHILIPPINES Anti-terror legislation has met with significant domestic and international criticism for its effects upon a wide range of civil liberties. Human rights supporters and political activists have been murdered and disappeared in the past, and many face the threat of arbitrary detention and ill-treatment. The prospect of armed conflict between the government and separatist Islamic groups persists.

POLAND The authorities have consistently denied any involvement in the special rendition process orchestrated by US authorities in the "war on terror". More generally, Poland has been criticized for inadequate measures taken to protect the rights of sexual minorities in Poland. The Polish parliament has also attracted UN criticism for its rejection of a law on gender equality.

PORTUGAL The police have been accused of numerous incidents of ill-treatment. Many of these have not been investigated.

QATAR The oil-rich Arab state of Qatar was elected to the UN Human Rights Council after having given assurances of continuing human rights reforms. Despite this, migrant workers face widespread discrimination and ill-treatment. Some convicted criminals are still sentenced to flogging, and numerous political prisoners are still being detained. State authorities have been criticized for failing to respond to widespread acts of violence against women.

ROMANIA The authorities have denied allegations of involvement in the special rendition of alleged terrorists. The Roma people face wide-ranging discrimination and persecution. The poor conditions of people living in long-term mental health institutions attract international criticism. Sexual minorities face systematic discrimination and persecution.

RUSSIA Lack of press freedom, and the tendency of state authorities to denounce dissent or criticism of the government as unpatriotic, are the foremost human rights concerns. Russia has been condemned by the European Court of Human Rights for the enforced disappearances of people during its military operations in Chechnya. Popular protest is subject to strict controls, and demonstrations have been broken up by the police amidst allegations of brutality. Human rights defenders and other activists face intimidation, harassment and violent assault. Racial minorities face widespread discrimination and lack adequate protection by the authorities. Incidences of torture as a means to extract confessions from detainees have been documented. Violence against women is widespread and is largely ignored by the authorities.

RWANDA Proceedings before the International Criminal Tribunal for Rwanda continue to pursue perpetrators of the 1994 genocide, but tensions between ethnic groups in Rwanda remain high. The widespread use of tribal councils jeopardizes the right to a fair trial. There are frequent allegations of torture and ill-treatment by the security services. Prison conditions have attracted international condemnation. Adult life expectancy is 45 years.

SAUDI ARABIA The kingdom's human rights record is very poor. Women are denied a number of fundamental freedoms, and discrimination against them is endemic. Arbitrary detention is high as are the number of detainees alleging torture and ill-treatment. Many alleged terrorists face indefinite periods of detention with no legal redress or prospect of a fair trial. Freedom of expression and assembly are tightly controlled. Many convicted criminals are punished in cruel and degrading ways, such as flogging or the severing of limbs. Freedom of religion is strictly limited and religious minorities have few, if any, legal protections.

SENEGAL The country is still attempting to overcome long periods of civil conflict. Opponents of the government, human rights supporters and independent journalists face concerted intimidation and the threat of violence. Torture has been documented in numerous places of detention.

SERBIA The status and future of Kosovo remains a central issue for the country. In addition, discrimination against various minority communities continues to attract international condemnation. The Serbian government has been consistently criticized for its apparent lack of co-operation in bringing to justice various individuals accused of committing atrocities and war crimes during the Bosnian war. The UN has also criticized Serbia for its lack of response to the high incidences of domestic violence. There are serious concerns over the trafficking of women into and out of Serbia.

SIERRA LEONE Decades of prolonged armed conflict appear to have come to an end, and progress has been made in the establishment of a truth and reconciliation commission. Nevertheless, the central problem remains the impoverishment of the population and poor access to healthcare. Adult life expectancy is 42 years – one of the lowest in the world. The rights of women are severely compromised, and state authorities have taken no action to reduce the very high percentage of girls undergoing female genital mutilation.

SINGAPORE State security legislation has been used to imprison numerous individuals suspected of involvement in terrorist activities without trial or access to lawyers. Freedom of expression and assembly are subject to limitations, with several organizations having been closed for "defamation" against the state.

SLOVAKIA The principal human rights issue in Slovakia concerns the widespread discrimination and persecution suffered by the Roma people. Other minority groups have also been subjected to violent attacks and have not received adequate protection from the police.

SLOVENIA The rights of the 20,000 so-called "erased" people continue to raise serious concerns. Most of them were born in other republics of the Former Yugoslavia, and had their permanent residency status in Slovenia revoked following the country's independence in 1991. Their access to social and economic benefits and other forms of legal protection have been severely affected as a consequence. In addition, Roma communities continue to face discrimination and persecution.

SOMALIA The humanitarian situation in this country is truly appalling. There has been no effective central government since 1992, and widespread violence and insecurity has claimed the lives of thousands of people. Thousands more are regularly detained by various militia groups. There is no effective rule of law, and a devastated public infrastructure denies many Somalis access to basic services. It is estimated that there are over 1 million internally displaced persons in Somalia, many living in appalling conditions. The rights of women are all but non-existent.

SOUTH AFRICA Despite the monumental achievement of overcoming apartheid, South Africa continues to suffer from a number of serious human rights issues. Widespread poverty is underlined by an adult life-expectancy of 51 years. Violent crime and murder are widespread and blight the lives of many South Africans. Violence against women and girls is also widespread. Political considerations continue to restrict the access of roughly half of HIV/AIDS sufferers to anti-retroviral drugs. Prison conditions are very poor and there are a number of reports of detainees being tortured.

SPAIN The response of police and security forces to Islamist and Basque terrorist atrocities has attracted significant criticism. Allegations have been made of torture and arbitrary detention. Asylum-seekers and migrants have been held in extra-territorial detention centres away from mainland Spain in conditions that have been internationally condemned.

SRI LANKA During the conflict between the Tamil Tigers and government forces, which was brought to an end in 2009, human rights abuses were endemic. Thousands of civilians lost their lives or suffered serious injury, and there were reports of hundreds of enforced disappearances and of torture. Hundreds of child soldiers were involved in the fighting. Severe restrictions were placed on elements of Sri Lankan civil society. It is too soon to evaluate whether Sri Lanka has genuinely entered a new, post-conflict stage.

SUDAN The country has one of the world's worst human rights records, beginning with the genocidal attacks made by government-supported militia on the people of Darfur. Violence against women and girls is widespread. There are countless reports of torture and ill-treatment. Severe restrictions have been imposed on freedom of expression, assembly, association and freedom of religion. Arbitrary detention is rife, and persistent concerns have been raised over lack of access to a fair trial.

SWAZILAND Crippling poverty remains the single greatest human rights concern in Swaziland. Adult life expectancy is 41 years. Two-thirds of the population live in absolute poverty and over a quarter of the population are infected with HIV. One third of children are either orphaned or are living with parents or carers who are too sick to care for them. Violence against women is widespread.

SWEDEN Considered by many to be a veritable human rights utopia, Sweden has been criticized by the UN for failing to accept Eritrean asylum-seekers.

SWITZERLAND The country has been criticized by the UN for failing to take adequate measures to combat growing racism and xenophobia in parts of Swiss society.

SYRIA A state of emergency has been in place since 1963, and presents the single greatest threat to human rights. There are hundreds of political prisoners, and many more are arbitrarily arrested and detained. Severe restrictions have been imposed on fundamental civil liberties. Allegations of torture are frequently made. Members of the Kurdish minority face systematic discrimination and persecution. Women continue to face widespread persecution and denial of basic rights.

TAIWAN The country has been criticized for laws restricting freedom of assembly and political demonstrations.

TAJIKISTAN Despite a relatively high adult life-expectancy of 66 years, Tajikistan suffers from a lack of valuable exports and a primarily mountainous terrain. Severe weather resulted in extensive food shortages in the winter of 2008/09. In addition, freedom of religion has been limited by government attacks on communities it considers unduly Islamist. Many Tajik males leave the country each year as labour migrants and experience severe discrimination and violation of their human rights in countries such as Russia and Kazakhstan. Violence against women is widespread and is mostly ignored by state authorities.

TANZANIA Adult life-expectancy in Tanzania is 51 years. In addition to the effects of poverty, the rights of women are widely violated with high levels of domestic violence and female genital mutilation. Refugees and migrants from neighbouring African countries have been subject to forcible return. Laws passed in 2007 have been criticized for placing undue restrictions upon the media.

THAILAND The country has suffered prolonged periods of political instability and intermittent bouts of martial law. Arbitrary detention is widespread and there are stringent restrictions on freedom of expression, association and assembly. A number of refugees from neighbouring countries have been forcibly returned. Continuing sex tourism exposes many women, girls and young boys to dangerous, demeaning and exploitative conditions.

TOGO Progress has been made towards establishing a system that is more effective at respecting human rights. Elections judged free and fair were held in 2007, and moves have been made towards bringing to justice persons accused of previously committing human rights violations. Despite this, restrictions on freedom of expression remain in force, and have been used to ban independent broadcasters critical of the present regime.

TRINIDAD & TOBAGO The principal human rights issue remains the behaviour of the police. Allegations of torture and ill-treatment whilst in custody are common, and have led to several deaths.

TUNISIA Allegations of torture and ill-treatment are widespread. Fundamental civil liberties, such as freedom of expression, association and assembly are subject to significant restrictions. A number of prosecutions of people accused of terrorism-related charges have been internationally condemned as resulting from unfair trials. Freedom of religion is also restricted and there are a number of reported cases of Muslim women being harassed for wearing the hijab.

TURKEY The country attracts domestic and international criticism for some aspects of its human rights record. Freedom of expression is restricted, as a means of protecting the Kemalist basis of the state. Women suffer widespread violence, and there are numerous reported cases of "honour killings" in both rural and urban areas of Turkey. Conflict continues between government forces and the Kurdish community in the Kurdish region, and civilians have lost their lives, livelihood and homes as a result. Allegations of torture are frequently made. Turkey continues largely to ignore a 2006 European Court of Human Rights judgement which ruled that its treatment of conscientious objectors to military service was illegal.

TURKMENISTAN The country is emerging from the idiosyncratic rule of its former president, who died in 2006. Despite proposals to establish various reforms of the political and legal system, human rights violations continue, particularly in the restriction and intimidation of political opponents. Freedom of expression and freedom of assembly are subject to strict controls. There are numerous reports of prisoners being held incommunicado for indefinite periods of time. Conscientious objectors have also faced persecution and imprisonment.

UGANDA Armed conflict between government forces and the Lord's Resistance Army has resulted in many deaths and human rights violations. Progress in peace talks has been slow. Freedom of expression is subject to wide-ranging restrictions. There are more than 1.5 million internally displaced persons living in camps in northern Uganda, who have sought refuge from armed conflict. Women are subject to high levels of violence and rape. Sexual minorities face systematic persecution and homosexuality remains a criminal offence.

UK The principal human rights concern is the government's response to the threat of terrorism. Individuals who have not been tried and convicted have been subject to so-called "control orders" that restrict their freedom of movement. The UK has also been criticized for deporting foreign nationals to countries where they face a credible threat of torture. The conditions in which failed asylum-seekers are kept prior to their removal has also attracted international criticism.

UKRAINE Allegations of torture and ill-treatment of those in police custody are frequently made. Refugees and asylum-seekers face the threat of forcible return. Relatively high levels of domestic violence and sex-trafficking violate women's rights. Members of racial, ethnic and religious minorities are frequently subjected to intimidation and harassment without adequate protection or redress.

UNITED ARAB EMIRATES Freedom of expression is subject to stringent controls, with a number of journalists and internet providers convicted of defamation for criticizing the regime. Migrant workers face persecution and exploitation. The trafficking of migrants for forced labour into the UAE continues to be largely ignored by authorities. Cruel and degrading punishments, such as flogging, continue to be meted out.

USA The administration of President Obama vowed, at the beginning of his term of office, to close the detention facilities at Guantánamo Bay. While this was met with widespread international approval, questions remained over the fate of the detainees. US military personnel have been accused, and in some cases convicted, of the murder, assault, and rape of civilians in countries such as Iraq and Afghanistan. US officials are alleged to have orchestrated and participated in so-called special rendition flights, and in the torture of suspected terrorists. Within the USA, over 50 million Americans do not have access to comprehensive medical treatment. A number of states in the US execute convicted criminals. The effects of the 2005 Hurricane Katrina continue to be felt by many of its victims, who remain internally displaced and lack permanent housing.

URUGUAY A number of welcome legal and political reforms have been made, but there has been little progress in bringing to justice the perpetrators of human rights violations carried out during the 1970s and 1980s. Uruguay has also been criticized for the large number of people being held in prisons who have yet to be convicted or sentenced.

UZBEKISTAN The country has attracted significant criticism for its poor human rights record. Allegations of torture are widespread. Freedom of expression, association and assembly are strictly curtailed. Religious freedom is subject to wide-ranging constraints. NGOs and civil society organizations are routinely subject to surveillance, intimidation and closure. The conditions of people working in Uzbekistan's extensive cotton industry are typically appalling and have attracted consistent criticism from the ILO and other organizations. Women are subject to high levels of violence, with little protection from the state. Corruption is rife among police and state officials.

VENEZUELA Political demonstrations are frequently met with violent policing tactics which have attracted significant criticism. President Hugo Chavez's powers have been the subject of much debate and discussion within Venezuela, and a proposal to extend his powers was rejected in a referendum in 2007.

Complaints against the police for ill-treatment and arbitrary detention have been steadily increasing.

VIETNAM Freedom of expression and association are subject to strict and wide-ranging controls. The judiciary sentences to death and executes relatively large numbers of people every year. Armed conflict between government forces and minority Shi'a Muslim communities occurs intermittently, with loss of civilian life and allegations of human rights abuses. Other ethnic minority communities face discrimination and persecution and, in some cases, have sought refuge in neighbouring Cambodia.

YEMEN Outbreaks of armed clashes and civil protest continue across the country. Poverty is widespread. There are frequent allegations of torture and ill-treatment. Fundamental civil liberties are subject to wide-ranging restrictions. There are numerous reports of political prisoners being held for long periods of time. Discrimination against women and girls takes many forms, including restricted access to basic education. Sentences of flogging are routinely handed out and administered without any opportunity of appeal.

ZAMBIA Adult life expectancy in Zambia is 41 years. In addition to the effects of extensive poverty and the under-developed public infrastructure, freedom of expression, assembly and association are subject to wide-ranging restrictions. Women and young girls face widespread discrimination and violence.

ZIMBABWE Adult life expectancy has fallen to 41 years. Despite the establishment of a coalition government in 2009, members of opposition parties continue to be subjected to assault and abductions. Human rights defenders have been subject to harassment and frequent death threats. There are reports of numerous extra-judicial killings. Allegations of torture are widespread. Severe restrictions on freedom of expression, assembly and association remain in place. Access to humanitarian aid has been restricted so as to exclude suspected opponents of the regime.

	1 Total population millions *2008 or latest available*	2 Gross National Income per capita current US$ *2008 or latest available*	3 Gini Index of wealth distribution* *2007*	4 Life Expectancy at birth *2008 or latest available*	5 Under-5 Mortality per 1,000 live births *2007*	6 Water % of population with access to improved source *2004–06*
Afghanistan	27.2	–	–	44	257	22%
Albania	3.1	7,950	31	77	15	97%
Algeria	34.4	7,940	35	72	37	85%
Angola	18	5,020	–	47	158	51%
Antigua and Barbuda	0.1	20,570	–	–	11	91%
Argentina	39.9	14,020	51	75	16	96%
Armenia	3.1	6,310	34	74	24	98%
Australia	21.4	34,040	35	81	6	100%
Austria	8.3	37,680	29	80	4	100%
Azerbaijan	8.7	7,770	37	67	39	78%
Bahamas	0.3	–		73	13	97%
Bahrain	0.8	27,210	–	76	10	0%
Bangladesh	160	1,440	33	66	61	80%
Barbados	0.3	18,600	–	77	12	100%
Belarus	9.7	12,150	30	70	13	100%
Belgium	10.7	34,760	33	80	5	0%
Belize	0.3	6,040	–	76	25	91%
Benin	8.7	1,460	37	62	123	65%
Bhutan	0.7	4,880	–	66	84	81%
Bolivia	9.7	4,140	60	66	57	86%
Bosnia and Herzegovina	3.8	8,620	26	75	14	99%
Botswana	1.9	13,100	61	51	40	96%
Brazil	192	10,070	57	73	22	91%
Brunei	0.4	50,200	–	77	9	0%
Bulgaria	7.6	11,950	29	73	12	99%
Burkina Faso	15.2	1,160	40	52	191	72%
Burma	49.2	1,290	–	62	103	80%
Burundi	8.1	380	42	51	180	71%
Cambodia	14.7	1,820	42	60	91	65%
Cameroon	18.9	2,180	45	50	148	70%
Canada	33.3	36,220	33	81	6	100%
Cape Verde	0.5	3,450	–	71	32	80%
Central African Republic	4.4	730	61	45	172	66%
Chad	11.1	1,160	–	51	209	48%
Chile	16.8	13,270	55	78	9	95%
China	1,325.60	6,020	47	73	22	88%
Colombia	44.5	8,510	59	73	20	93%
Comoros	0.6	1,170	–	65	66	85%
Congo	3.6	3,090	–	54	125	71%
Congo, Dem. Rep.	64.2	290	–	46	161	46%
Cook Islands	0.01	9,100	–	74	–	95%
Costa Rica	4.5	10,950	50	79	11	98%
Côte d'Ivoire	20.6	1,580	45	58	127	81%
Croatia	4.4	18,420	29	76	6	99%
Cuba	11.2	–	–	78	7	91%
Cyprus	0.9	24,040	–	79	5	100%
Czech Republic	10.4	22,790	25	77	4	100%
Denmark	5.5	37,280	25	78	4	100%

114

*0 = absolute equality;
100 = absolute inequality

7 Primary education % enrolled *latest available* 2000–07			8 Secondary education % enrolled *latest available* 2000–07			9 Refugees by country of origin	10 Internally Displaced Persons	11 Press Freedom Index**	12 Freedom to Associate Index†	
boys	*girls*	*total*	*boys*	*girls*	*total*	*2008*	*2008*	*2009*	*2007*	
74%	46%	61%	–	–	–	2,833,128	230,670	54.25	4	Afghanistan
94%	93%	94%	74%	72%	73%	15,006	–	21.75	8	Albania
96%	94%	95%	65%	68%	66%	9,060	–	49.56	6	Algeria
–	–	–	–	–	–	171,393	–	36.50	6	Angola
–	–	–	–	–	–	26	–	–	9	Antigua and Barbuda
99%	98%	99%	75%	82%	78%	1,047	–	11.33	11	Argentina
80%	84%	82%	84%	88%	86%	16,336	–	31.13	5	Armenia
96%	97%	96%	87%	88%	87%	43	–	3.13	12	Australia
97%	98%	97%	–	–	–	14	–	3.00	12	Austria
86%	83%	85%	79%	76%	78%	16,319	603,251	53.50	3	Azerbaijan
87%	89%	88%	83%	85%	84%	15	–	–	12	Bahamas
98%	98%	98%	91%	96%	93%	80	–	36.50	3	Bahrain
87%	91%	89%	40%	42%	41%	10,098	–	37.33	6	Bangladesh
97%	96%	96%	88%	89%	89%	34	–	–	12	Barbados
90%	89%	89%	87%	89%	88%	5,384	–	59.50	0	Belarus
97%	98%	97%	89%	85%	87%	61	–	2.50	12	Belgium
97%	97%	97%	64%	70%	67%	20	–	–	11	Belize
87%	73%	80%	23%	11%	17%	318	–	16.00	12	Benin
79%	79%	79%	38%	39%	39%	104,965	–	15.75	3	Bhutan
95%	95%	95%	72%	70%	71%	454	–	24.17	10	Bolivia
–	–	–	–	–	–	74,366	124,529	10.50	8	Bosnia and Herzegovina
83%	85%	84%	52%	60%	56%	26	–	15.50	10	Botswana
94%	95%	94%	75%	83%	79%	1,404	–	15.88	10	Brazil
94%	94%	94%	88%	92%	90%	1	–	63.50	3	Brunei
93%	92%	92%	90%	88%	89%	3,040	–	15.61	11	Bulgaria
52%	42%	47%	14%	10%	12%	725	–	15.00	9	Burkina Faso
99%	100%	100%	46%	46%	46%	184,413	67,290	102.67	0	Burma
76%	73%	75%	–	–	–	281,592	100,000	29.00	5	Burundi
91%	89%	90%	33%	28%	31%	17,253	–	35.17	6	Cambodia
–	–	–	–	–	–	13,870	–	30.50	3	Cameroon
99%	100%	100%	–	–	–	101	–	3.70	12	Canada
88%	87%	88%	56%	63%	59%	30	–	11.00	11	Cape Verde
53%	38%	46%	13%	9%	11%	125,106	197,000	17.75	6	Central African Republic
71%	50%	60%	16%	5%	11%	55,105	166,718	44.50	4	Chad
–	–	–	–	–	–	994	–	10.50	12	Chile
99%	99%	99%	–	–	–	175,180	–	84.50	2	China
89%	88%	89%	62%	69%	65%	373,532	3,000,000	40.13	6	Colombia
75%	71%	73%	15%	15%	15%	378	–	19.00	6	Comoros
58%	52%	55%	–	–	–	19,925	–	34.25	7	Congo
–	–	–	–	–	–	367,995	1,460,102	53.50	5	Congo, Dem. Rep.
73%	75%	74%	62%	68%	64%	–	–	–	–	Cook Islands
91%	93%	92%	58%	64%	61%	354	–	8.00	11	Costa Rica
61%	49%	55%	25%	14%	20%	22,227	683,956	29.00	4	Côte d'Ivoire
91%	90%	90%	86%	88%	87%	97,012	2,497	17.17	12	Croatia
96%	97%	97%	86%	88%	87%	7,938	–	94.00	1	Cuba
99%	99%	99%	93%	95%	94%	10	–	5.50	12	Cyprus
91%	94%	93%	–	–	–	1,358	–	5.00	12	Czech Republic
95%	96%	96%	88%	90%	89%	11	–	0.00	12	Denmark

** low score = freedom; high score = lack of freedom
† 0 = lack of freedom; 12 = total freedom

	1 Total population millions *2008 or latest available*	2 Gross National Income per capita current US$ *2008 or latest available*	3 Gini Index of wealth distribution* *2007*	4 Life Expectancy at birth *2008 or latest available*	5 Under-5 Mortality per 1,000 live births *2007*	6 Water % of population with access to improved source *2004–06*
Djibouti	0.8	2,330	–	55	127	92%
Dominica	0.1	8,300	–	–	11	97%
Dominican Republic	9.8	7,890	52	72	38	95%
East Timor	1.1	4,690	–	61	97	62%
Ecuador	13.5	7,760	54	75	22	95%
Egypt	81.5	5,460	34	70	36	98%
El Salvador	6.1	6,670	52	71	24	84%
Equatorial Guinea	0.7	21,700	–	50	206	43%
Eritrea	5	630	–	58	70	60%
Estonia	1.3	19,280	36	73	6	100%
Ethiopia	80.7	870	30	55	119	42%
Fiji	0.8	4,270	–	69	18	47%
Finland	5.3	35,660	27	79	4	100%
France	62	34,400	33	81	4	100%
Gabon	1.4	12,270	–	61	91	87%
Gambia	1.7	1,280	50	56	109	86%
Georgia	4.4	4,850	40	71	30	99%
Germany	82.1	35,940	28	80	4	100%
Ghana	23.4	1,430	41	57	115	80%
Greece	11.2	28,470	34	80	4	100%
Grenada	0.1	8,060	–	69	19	95%
Guatemala	13.7	4,690	55	70	39	96%
Guinea	9.8	1,190	39	58	150	70%
Guinea-Bissau	1.6	530	47	48	198	57%
Guyana	0.8	2,510	–	67	60	93%
Haiti	9.8	1,180	59	61	76	58%
Honduras	7.2	3,870	54	70	24	84%
Hungary	10	17,790	27	73	7	100%
Iceland	0.3	25,220	–	81	3	100%
India	1,140.00	2,960	37	65	72	89%
Indonesia	228.2	3,830	34	71	31	80%
Iran	72	10,840	43	71	33	94%
Iraq	28.9	–	–	68	44	77%
Ireland	4.5	37,350	34	79	4	0%
Israel	7.3	27,450	39	81	5	100%
Italy	59.9	30,250	36	81	4	0%
Jamaica	2.7	7,360	46	73	31	93%
Japan	127.7	35,220	25	83	4	100%
Jordan	5.9	5,530	39	73	24	98%
Kazakhstan	15.7	9,690	34	66	32	96%
Kenya	38.5	1,580	43	54	121	57%
Kiribati	0.1	3,660	–	–	63	65%
Korea, North	23.9	–	–	67	55	100%
Korea, South	48.6	28,120	32	79	5	92%
Kuwait	2.7	52,610	–	78	11	0%
Kyrgyzstan	5.3	2,140	30	68	38	89%
Laos	6.2	2,040	35	65	70	60%
Latvia	2.3	16,740	38	71	9	99%

*0 = absolute equality;
100 = absolute inequality

7 Primary education % enrolled latest available 2000–07			8 Secondary education % enrolled latest available 2000–07			9 Refugees by country of origin	10 Internally Displaced Persons	11 Press Freedom Index**	12 Freedom to Associate Index†	
boys	girls	total	boys	girls	total	2008	2008	2009	2007	
42%	34%	38%	26%	17%	22%	650	–	31.00	5	Djibouti
75%	80%	77%	77%	85%	81%	56	–	–	12	Dominica
77%	79%	78%	47%	57%	52%	318	–	26.83	11	Dominican Republic
70%	67%	68%	–	–	23%	7	15,860	16.00	7	East Timor
96%	97%	97%	57%	58%	57%	1,066	–	20.00	11	Ecuador
98%	94%	96%	82%	78%	80%	6,780	–	51.38	2	Egypt
94%	94%	94%	53%	56%	54%	5,151	–	17.25	8	El Salvador
91%	83%	87%	–	–	25%	384	–	65.50	0	Equatorial Guinea
50%	43%	47%	30%	20%	25%	186,398	–	115.50	0	Eritrea
95%	94%	94%	90%	92%	91%	248	–	0.50	12	Estonia
74%	69%	71%	29%	19%	24%	63,878	–	49.00	3	Ethiopia
91%	91%	91%	76%	83%	79%	1,868	–	60.00	4	Fiji
97%	97%	97%	96%	96%	96%	4	–	0.00	12	Finland
98%	99%	99%	98%	100%	99%	101	–	10.67	12	France
88%	88%	88%	–	–	–	129	–	43.50	6	Gabon
59%	64%	62%	40%	37%	38%	1,352	–	48.25	6	Gambia
88%	91%	89%	77%	81%	79%	12,598	293,048	18.83	7	Georgia
98%	98%	98%	–	–	–	166	–	3.50	12	Germany
73%	71%	72%	47%	43%	45%	13,242	–	6.00	11	Ghana
100%	99%	100%	92%	93%	92%	67	–	9.00	11	Greece
84%	83%	84%	78%	80%	79%	312	–	–	9	Grenada
96%	92%	94%	40%	37%	38%	5,934	–	29.50	8	Guatemala
77%	66%	72%	35%	20%	28%	9,495	–	28.50	5	Guinea
53%	37%	45%	11%	6%	9%	1,065	–	23.50	8	Guinea-Bissau
–	–	–	–	–	–	708	–	10.50	10	Guyana
–	–	–	–	–	–	23,066	–	15.00	6	Haiti
96%	97%	96%	–	–	–	1,116	–	42.00	8	Honduras
89%	88%	88%	90%	90%	90%	1,614	–	5.50	12	Hungary
98%	97%	98%	89%	91%	90%	7	–	2.00	12	Iceland
90%	87%	89%	–	–	–	19,569	–	29.33	10	India
97%	94%	96%	59%	59%	59%	19,345	–	28.50	9	Indonesia
91%	100%	94%	79%	75%	77%	69,061	–	104.14	2	Iran
95%	82%	89%	45%	32%	38%	1,903,519	2,647,251	53.30	3	Iraq
95%	95%	95%	85%	90%	87%	7	–	0.00	12	Ireland
96%	98%	97%	88%	89%	89%	1,494	–	23.75	12	Israel
99%	98%	99%	93%	94%	94%	62	–	12.14	12	Italy
90%	90%	90%	77%	80%	78%	826	–	4.75	9	Jamaica
100%	100%	100%	99%	99%	99%	185	–	3.25	10	Japan
89%	91%	90%	81%	83%	82%	1,890	–	31.88	5	Jordan
90%	90%	90%	86%	86%	86%	4,825	–	49.67	4	Kazakhstan
75%	76%	76%	43%	42%	42%	9,688	404,000	25.00	9	Kenya
96%	98%	97%	65%	72%	68%	38	–	–	12	Kiribati
–	–	–	–	–	–	886	–	112.50	0	Korea, North
100%	93%	98%	99%	93%	96%	1,104	–	15.67	11	Korea, South
84%	83%	84%	75%	79%	77%	854	–	15.25	6	Kuwait
86%	85%	86%	80%	81%	81%	2,517	–	40.00	7	Kyrgyzstan
86%	81%	84%	38%	32%	35%	8,598	–	92.00	1	Laos
89%	92%	90%	–	–	–	763	–	3.00	12	Latvia

** low score = freedom; high score = lack of freedom   117
† 0 = lack of freedom; 12 = total freedom

	1 Total population millions 2008 or latest available	2 Gross National Income per capita current US$ 2008 or latest available	3 Gini Index of wealth distribution* 2007	4 Life Expectancy at birth 2008 or latest available	5 Under-5 Mortality per 1,000 live births 2007	6 Water % of population with access to improved source 2004–06
Lebanon	4.1	10,880	–	72	29	100%
Lesotho	2	2,000	63	43	84	78%
Liberia	3.8	300	–	58	133	64%
Libya	6.3	15,630	–	74	18	0%
Lithuania	3.4	18,210	36	71	8	0%
Luxembourg	0.5	64,320	–	79	3	100%
Macedonia	2	9,950	39	74	17	100%
Madagascar	19.1	1,040	48	61	112	47%
Malawi	14.3	830	39	48	111	76%
Malaysia	27	13,740	49	74	11	99%
Maldives	0.3	5,280	–	68	30	83%
Mali	12.7	1,090	40	54	196	60%
Malta	0.4	22,460	–	80	5	100%
Marshall Islands	0.1	–	–	–	54	87%
Mauritania	3.2	2,000	39	64	119	60%
Mauritius	1.3	12,480	–	72	15	100%
Mexico	106.4	14,270	46	75	35	95%
Micronesia, Fed. Sts.	0.1	3,000	–	69	40	94%
Moldova	3.6	3,210	33	69	18	92%
Mongolia	2.6	3,480	33	67	43	72%
Montenegro	0.6	13,920	–	74	10	98%
Morocco	31.2	4,330	40	71	34	83%
Mozambique	21.8	770	47	42	168	42%
Namibia	2.1	6,270	74	53	68	93%
Nauru	–	–	–	–	–	0%
Nepal	28.6	1,120	47	64	55	89%
Netherlands	16.4	41,670	31	80	5	100%
New Zealand	4.3	25,090	36	80	6	0%
Nicaragua	5.7	2,620	43	73	35	79%
Niger	14.7	680	51	57	176	42%
Nigeria	151.3	1,940	44	47	189	47%
Niue	–	–	–	–	–	0%
Norway	4.8	58,500	26	80	4	100%
Oman	2.8	20,650	–	76	12	0%
Pakistan	166	2,700	31	65	90	90%
Palau	0.02	–	–	–	10	89%
Palestine Authority	3.8	–	–	73	27	89%
Panama	3.4	11,650	56	76	23	92%
Papua New Guinea	6.4	2,000	51	57	65	40%
Paraguay	6.2	4,820	58	72	29	77%
Peru	28.8	7,980	52	73	20	84%
Philippines	90.3	3,900	45	72	28	93%
Poland	38.1	17,310	35	75	7	0%
Portugal	10.6	22,080	39	78	4	99%
Puerto Rico	4	–	–	78	–	0%
Qatar	1.3	–	–	76	15	100%
Romania	21.5	13,500	31	73	15	88%
Russia	141.8	15,630	40	68	15	97%

*0 = absolute equality;
100 = absolute inequality

7 Primary education % enrolled latest available 2000–07			8 Secondary education % enrolled latest available 2000–07			9 Refugees by country of origin	10 Internally Displaced Persons	11 Press Freedom Index**	12 Freedom to Associate Index†	
boys	girls	total	boys	girls	total	2008	2008	2009	2007	
82%	82%	82%	70%	77%	73%	12,967	–	15.42	8	Lebanon
71%	74%	72%	19%	29%	24%	8	–	27.50	7	Lesotho
40%	39%	40%	22%	13%	17%	75,213	–	15.50	8	Liberia
–	–	–	–	–	–	2,084	–	64.50	0	Libya
90%	89%	89%	92%	93%	92%	490	–	2.25	11	Lithuania
96%	98%	97%	82%	86%	84%	–	–	4.00	12	Luxembourg
92%	92%	92%	82%	80%	81%	7,521	–	8.75	7	Macedonia
96%	96%	96%	17%	18%	17%	277	–	45.83	8	Madagascar
88%	94%	91%	25%	23%	24%	106	–	15.50	8	Malawi
100%	100%	100%	66%	72%	69%	608	–	44.25	5	Malaysia
97%	97%	97%	65%	70%	67%	16	–	14.00	4	Maldives
68%	54%	61%	–	–	–	1,758	–	8.00	9	Mali
92%	91%	91%	84%	90%	87%	9	–	2.50	12	Malta
67%	66%	66%	43%	47%	45%	–	–	–	–	Marshall Islands
78%	82%	80%	16%	15%	16%	45,601	–	28.50	8	Mauritania
94%	96%	95%	81%	82%	82%	24	–	14.00	12	Mauritius
98%	97%	98%	71%	70%	70%	6,162	–	48.25	9	Mexico
–	–	92%	–	–	25%	–	–	–	–	Micronesia, Fed. Sts.
88%	88%	88%	80%	83%	81%	5,555	–	33.75	6	Moldova
90%	93%	91%	77%	87%	82%	1,333	–	23.33	10	Mongolia
–	–	–	–	–	–	1,283	–	17.00	10	Montenegro
91%	85%	88%	37%	32%	35%	3,533	–	41.00	6	Morocco
79%	73%	76%	4%	4%	4%	208	–	19.00	7	Mozambique
74%	79%	76%	30%	40%	35%	985	–	9.00	12	Namibia
–	–	60%	–	–	58%	3	–	–	–	Nauru
91%	87%	89%	–	–	–	4,189	–	35.63	6	Nepal
99%	97%	98%	88%	89%	88%	46	–	1.00	12	Netherlands
99%	99%	99%	91%	93%	92%	10	–	3.00	–	New Zealand
90%	90%	90%	40%	47%	43%	1,537	–	16.75	7	Nicaragua
56%	40%	48%	12%	7%	9%	796	–	48.50	8	Niger
68%	59%	63%	28%	23%	26%	14,169	–	46.00	8	Nigeria
–	–	90%	91%	96%	93%	–	–	–	–	Niue
98%	98%	98%	96%	97%	96%	4	–	0.00	12	Norway
73%	75%	74%	78%	77%	77%	56	–	29.50	3	Oman
74%	57%	66%	33%	26%	30%	32,403	155,809	65.67	4	Pakistan
98%	95%	96%	–	–	–	1	–	–	11	Palau
76%	76%	76%	87%	92%	90%	340,016	–	69.83	–	Palestine Authority
99%	98%	99%	61%	68%	64%	111	–	14.50	11	Panama
–	–	–	–	–	–	46	–	14.70	9	Papua New Guinea
94%	95%	94%	56%	59%	57%	101	–	14.33	8	Paraguay
96%	97%	96%	72%	72%	72%	7,339	–	20.88	8	Peru
91%	93%	91%	55%	66%	60%	1,354	–	38.25	8	Philippines
96%	96%	96%	93%	94%	94%	2,391	–	9.50	12	Poland
98%	98%	98%	78%	86%	82%	36	–	8.00	12	Portugal
0%	0%	0%	0%	0%	0%	–	–	–	–	Puerto Rico
93%	94%	94%	91%	90%	91%	71	–	24.00	2	Qatar
93%	93%	93%	74%	73%	73%	4,756	–	12.50	11	Romania
91%	91%	91%	–	–	–	103,061	91,505	60.88	4	Russia

** low score = freedom; high score = lack of freedom   **119**
† 0 = lack of freedom; 12 = total freedom

	1 Total population millions 2008 or latest available	2 Gross National Income per capita current US$ 2008 or latest available	3 Gini Index of wealth distribution* 2007	4 Life Expectancy at birth 2008 or latest available	5 Under-5 Mortality per 1,000 live births 2007	6 Water % of population with access to improved source 2004–06
Rwanda	9.7	1,010	47	50	181	65%
St. Kitts and Nevis	0.05	15,170	–	–	18	99%
St. Lucia	0.2	9,190	–	74	18	98%
St. Vincent and Grenadines	0.1	8,770	–	72	19	0%
Samoa	0.2	4,340	–	72	27	88%
São Tomé and Principe	0.2	1,780	–	65	99	86%
Saudi Arabia	24.6	22,950	–	73	25	0%
Senegal	12.2	1,760	41	55	114	77%
Serbia	7.4	11,150	–	73	8	99%
Seychelles	0.1	19,770	–	73	13	88%
Sierra Leone	5.6	750	63	48	262	53%
Singapore	4.8	47,940	43	80	3	100%
Slovakia	5.4	21,300	26	74	8	100%
Slovenia	2	26,910	28	78	4	0%
Solomon Islands	0.5	2,580	–	64	70	70%
Somalia	9	–	–	48	142	29%
South Africa	48.7	9,780	58	50	59	93%
Spain	45.6	31,130	35	81	4	100%
Sri Lanka	20.2	4,460	40	72	21	82%
Sudan	41.3	1,930	–	58	109	70%
Suriname	0.5	7,130	–	69	29	92%
Swaziland	1.2	5,010	50	46	91	60%
Sweden	9.2	38,180	25	81	3	100%
Switzerland	7.6	46,460	34	82	5	100%
Syria	21.2	4,350	–	74	17	89%
Tajikistan	6.8	1,860	33	67	67	67%
Tanzania	42.5	1,230	35	56	116	55%
Thailand	67.4	5,990	42	69	7	98%
Togo	6.5	820	–	63	100	59%
Tonga	0.1	3,880	–	72	23	100%
Trinidad and Tobago	1.3	23,950	39	70	35	94%
Tunisia	10.3	7,070	40	74	21	94%
Turkey	73.9	13,770	44	72	23	97%
Turkmenistan	5	6,210	41	63	50	72%
Tuvalu	–	–	–	–	–	93%
Uganda	31.7	1,140	46	53	130	64%
Ukraine	46.3	7,210	28	68	24	97%
United Arab Emirates	4.5	45,510	–	79	8	100%
United Kingdom	61.4	36,130	36	79	6	100%
United States	304.1	46,970	41	78	8	99%
Uruguay	3.3	12,540	45	76	14	100%
Uzbekistan	27.3	2,660	37	67	41	88%
Vanuatu	0.2	3,940	–	70	34	60%
Venezuela	27.9	12,830	48	74	19	83%
Vietnam	86.2	2,700	34	74	15	92%
Yemen	23.1	2,210	33	63	73	66%
Zambia	12.6	1,230	51	46	170	58%
Zimbabwe	12.5	–	50	45	90	81%

*0 = absolute equality;
100 = absolute inequality

7 Primary education % enrolled latest available 2000–07			8 Secondary education % enrolled latest available 2000–07			9 Refugees by country of origin	10 Internally Displaced Persons	11 Press Freedom Index**	12 Freedom to Associate Index†	
boys	girls	total	boys	girls	total	2008	2008	2009	2007	
76%	81%	79%	–	–	10%	72,530	–	64.67	3	Rwanda
64%	78%	71%	70%	61%	65%	4	–	–	12	St. Kitts and Nevis
99%	97%	98%	65%	80%	73%	288	–	–	–	St. Lucia
93%	88%	90%	57%	71%	64%	750	–	–	11	St. Vincent and Grenadines
90%	91%	90%	62%	71%	66%	4	–	–	10	Samoa
97%	98%	98%	31%	34%	33%	35	–	–	10	São Tomé and Principe
–	–	–	–	–	–	712	–	76.50	0	Saudi Arabia
71%	70%	71%	23%	18%	20%	16,006	–	22.00	10	Senegal
95%	95%	95%	–	–	76%	185,935	225,879	15.50	11	Serbia
99%	100%	99%	94%	100%	94%	53	–	16.00	9	Seychelles
–	–	–	27%	19%	23%	32,536	–	34.00	8	Sierra Leone
–	–	–	–	–	–	109	–	45.00	3	Singapore
92%	92%	92%	–	–	–	331	–	11.00	12	Slovakia
96%	95%	95%	90%	91%	90%	52	–	9.50	12	Slovenia
62%	62%	62%	29%	25%	27%	52	–	–	9	Solomon Islands
–	–	–	–	–	–	561,154	1,277,200	77.50	0	Somalia
88%	88%	88%	59%	66%	62%	453	–	8.50	12	South Africa
100%	99%	100%	92%	96%	94%	27	–	11.00	12	Spain
98%	97%	98%	–	–	–	137,752	504,800	75.00	8	Sri Lanka
45%	37%	41%	–	–	–	419,248	1,201,040	54.00	3	Sudan
95%	98%	96%	57%	79%	68%	50	–	10.60	11	Suriname
78%	79%	78%	29%	35%	32%	32	–	52.50	3	Swaziland
95%	95%	95%	99%	99%	99%	15	–	0.00	12	Sweden
89%	89%	89%	84%	80%	82%	32	–	1.00	12	Switzerland
97%	92%	95%	64%	61%	63%	15,211	–	78.00	0	Syria
99%	95%	97%	87%	74%	80%	544	–	32.00	–	Tajikistan
98%	97%	97%	22%	20%	21%	1,270	–	15.50	7	Tanzania
95%	94%	94%	68%	75%	71%	1,815	–	44.00	5	Thailand
86%	75%	80%	30%	14%	22%	16,750	–	15.50	6	Togo
98%	94%	96%	54%	68%	60%	7	–	–	5	Tonga
85%	85%	85%	64%	67%	65%	231	–	7.00	11	Trinidad and Tobago
96%	97%	96%	61%	68%	65%	2,349	–	61.50	2	Tunisia
93%	89%	91%	74%	64%	69%	214,378	–	38.25	7	Turkey
–	–	–	–	–	–	736	–	107.00	0	Turkmenistan
–	–	100%	–	–	–	2	–	–	12	Tuvalu
–	–	–	16%	14%	15%	7,548	853,000	21.50	6	Uganda
90%	90%	90%	83%	84%	84%	28,424	–	22.00	10	Ukraine
88%	88%	88%	78%	80%	79%	256	–	21.50	3	United Arab Emirates
98%	99%	98%	91%	94%	92%	185	–	4.00	12	United Kingdom
91%	93%	92%	88%	88%	88%	2,137	–	4.00	11	United States
100%	100%	100%	–	–	–	199	–	7.63	12	Uruguay
–	–	–	–	–	–	6,308	–	67.67	0	Uzbekistan
88%	86%	87%	41%	35%	38%	–	–	–	11	Vanuatu
91%	91%	91%	62%	71%	66%	5,807	–	39.50	6	Venezuela
–	–	95%	–	–	61%	328,183	–	81.67	2	Vietnam
85%	65%	75%	49%	26%	37%	1,777	100,000	83.38	4	Yemen
90%	94%	92%	31%	25%	28%	195	–	26.75	8	Zambia
87%	88%	88%	38%	36%	37%	16,841	–	46.50	2	Zimbabwe

** low score = freedom; high score = lack of freedom   121
† 0 = lack of freedom; 12 = total freedom

Sources

For sources that are available on the internet, in most cases only the root address has been given. To view the source, it is recommended that the reader types the title of the page or document into Google or another search engine.

Major Human Rights Treaties
United Nations Treaty Collection. http://treaties.un.org

Part 1: State, Identity & Citizenship

18–19 Political Rights
Smith D. *The state of the world atlas*. Berkeley: University of California Press and London: Earthscan. 2008. pp.78-79.
BBC News Country Profiles http://news.bbc.co.uk
Foreign and Commonwealth Office. *Annual report on human rights 2008*. www.fco.gov.uk

20–21 Citizenship
Right to Vote
Central Intelligence Agency. The World Factbook. www.cia.gov [Accessed 2009 Sept 30.]

... 33% of people
UNDP. *Human development report 2002: deepening democracy in a fragmented world*. Table 1.1. http://hdr.undp.org

Voter Turnout
Institute for Democracy and Electoral Assistance. www.idea.int [Accessed 2009 Oct 5.]

...only 57% of Americans
United States Election Project. http://elections.gmu.edu

22–23 Wealth & Inequality
Inequality
World Bank. World Development Indicators. www.wri.org
www.forbes.com
UNDP. *Human development report 2007/08*. Table 3. Human and income poverty: developing countries. http://hdr.undp.org

Division of Wealth
The World Bank. *World Bank development report 2007/08*. Table 2.7.
http://siteresources.worldbank.org

...Poverty accounts for
www.bread.org

24–25 Quality of Life
Relative Human Development
UNDP. *Human development report 2007/08*. Table 1. http://hdr.undp.org

... 16,000 children die
www.bread.org

Drinking Water
UNICEF and WHO Joint Monitoring Programme for Water Supply and Sanitation. *Progress on drinking water and sanitation*. New York: UNICEF and Geneva: WHO. 2008.
JMP Statistical database. www.wssinfo.org

Lack of Food
Food and Agriculture Organization. Food Security Statistics. www.fao.org

26–27 Health
Education for Life
National Vital Statistics report. vol. 57, no. 14. 2009 April 17. p. 12.

Links Between Human Rights and Health
Based on WHO diagram.

Healthy Life
WHO. *World health statistics report 2009*. Table 1. Summary. p. 44. www.who.int

Education and Health
WHO. *World health statistics report 2009*. Table 8. Health inequities. p. 119. www.who.int

Smoking in Public Places
WHO report on the global tobacco epidemic, 2008: The MPOWER package. Geneva: World Health Organization. 2008. www.tobaccoatlas.org

Part 2: Judicial Violations & Legal Restrictions

30–31 Torture
UN Special Rapporteur on Torture. www.unhchr.ch
European Committee for the Prevention of Torture. *18th general report on the CPT's activities, 2007-08*. Strasbourg: Council of Europe. 2008.
Amnesty International. *The state of the world's human rights 2008*. www.amnesty.org
Foreign & Commonwealth Office. *Annual report on human rights 2008*. www.fco.gov.uk
Human Rights Watch. *World report 2009*. www.hrw.org

Torturers
Amnesty International. 2008. op. cit.
Foreign & Commonwealth Office. 2008. op. cit.

32–33 Arbitrary Detention
Amnesty International. *The state of the world's human rights 2008*. www.amnesty.org
Foreign & Commonwealth Office. *Annual report on human rights 2008*. www.fco.gov.uk
Human Rights Watch. *World report 2009*. www.hrw.org
Dui Hua Foundation. www.duihua.org

34–35 Capital Punishment
International Instruments against Death Penalty
... death sentences in USA
Amnesty International USA. *Death penalty facts*. Updated 2009 Aug. www.amnestyusa.org/abolish

Death Penalty
Death penalty: Countries abolitionist for all crimes. www.amnesty.org
Death penalty banned in New Mexico. *The Daily Beast*. 2009 Sept 24. www.thedailybeast.com

...In 2008, at least 2,390
Amnesty International (USA). Death Sentences & Executions in 2008. www.amnesty.org

36–37 Policing
Discriminatory Policing
2000/01 and 2002/03 data from: Metropolitan Police Authority. Report of the MPA scrutiny on MPA stop and search practice. www.mpa.gov.uk
2004/05 data from: Ministry of Justice. Statistics on race and criminal justice system 2005. www.statewatch.org
2006/07 data from: Ministry of Justice. Statistics on race and criminal justice system 2006/7. 2008 July. www.justice.gov.uk

Police Violations of Human Rights
Bahamas, Bangladesh, Cote d'Ivoire, India, Kenya
Amnesty International. *Amnesty International Report 2009*. http://thereport.amnesty.org [Accessed 2009 Sept.]

UK
Open verdict at Menezes inquest. 2008 Dec 12. http://news.bbc.co.uk

USA tasers
United Nations Committee on the Elimination of Racial Discrimination. *In the shadows of the war on terror:*

persistent police brutality and abuse of people of color in the United States. 2007 Dec. www2.ohchr.org. Cites Sherman S. Amnesty International: US taser deaths up. Associated Press. 2006 Mar 27.

USA assault
Crisis of confidence: persistent problems within the New Orleans Police Department: voices and solutions from communities most impacted by violent crime. Safe Streets/Strong Communities. 2006 Oct. www.safestreetsnola.org

Syria
Human Rights Watch. *World report 2008.* p. 522. www.hrw.org

Part 3: Freedom of Expression

40–41 Freedom of Speech
The Committee to Protect Journalists. CPJ's prison census: online and in jail. 2008 Dec 1. http://cpj.org
Reporters Without Borders.World Press Freedom Index 2009. www.rsf.org

Media Freedom Under Threat

Abuse of Journalists
Reporters Without Borders. www.rsf.org
Russia: Panos Pictures
Obituary: Natalia Estemirova. 2009 July 15. http://news.bbc.co.uk
Afghanistan Parwiz Kambakhsh www.rawa.org

Media
Committee to Protect Journalists. http://cpj.org

42–43 Communications Censorship

Internet Censorship
Colour: http://map.opennet.net/filtering-pol.html
Symbol: RSF. Internet enemies. 2009 Mar 12. www.rsf.org
Saudi Arabia, South Korea, Switzerland, Uzbekistan
http://opennet.net
Burma
www.rsf.org
China
Heacock R. China shuts down internet in Xinjiang region after riots. http://opennet.net
Watts J. China thinks twice – and its 300m internet users scent a rare victory. 2009 June 30. www.guardian.co.uk
Iran
Watts J. op. cit.

Tunisia
Gharbia Sami Ben. Facebook user jailed for spreading rumours liable to disrupt public order. 2009 July 7. http://advocacy.globalvoicesonline.org
Turkey
Anderson K. Net surveillance and filters are a reality for Europe, too. 2009 June 24. www.guardian.co.uk

Media Outlets Closed
...1,740 websites
RSF press freedom round up 2008. www.rsf.org

44-45 Assembly and Association

Freedom of Association under Threat
Freedom House www.freedomhouse.org

Belarus
Article 19. Violation of freedom of assembly and use of force against peaceful demonstrators. 2009 Feb 19. Cited on: www.unhcr.org/refworld
Jordan, Kyrgyzstan, Singapore
Amnesty International. *The state of the world's human rights 2008.* www.amnesty.org
China, Equatorial Guinea, USA, Zimbabwe
ITUC. *Annual survey of violation of human rights, 2008.* http://survey08.ituc-csi.org

Part 4: Conflict & Migration

48–49 Genocide
Genocide Intervention Network www.genocideintervention.net
Genocide Watch www.genocidewatch.org
UNHCR www.unhcr.org

20th-century Genocides
Genocide Watch www.genocidewatch.org/campaigntoendgenocide/about.html

50–51 War & Armed Conflict

War at Home
...more than 2 million
Human Security Report Project. *Mini atlas of human security.* Washington DC: The World Bank, Vancouver: Human Security Report Project. 2008. pp.12-16. Based on data from UCDP/PRIO.

Non-State Conflict
Human Security Report Project. op. cit. pp. 22-23. Based on data from UCDP/HSRP.

Legal Status of Gulf Wars
Timeline: Iraq. news.bbc.co.uk
World Press Review Online. The United Nations, international law, and the war in Iraq. www.worldpress.org
No-fly zones: the legal position. 2001 Feb 19. http://news.bbc.co.uk
Richardson J. editor. *Iraq and weapons of mass destruction.* National Security Archive Electronic Briefing Book. no. 80. Updated 2004 Feb 11. George Washington University. www.gwu.edu
Weapons of mass destruction. Iraq Survey Group final report. Global Security. www.globalsecurity.org

52–53 Arms Trade

Persistent Killers
International Campaign to Ban Landmines. *Landmine monitor report 2008: toward a mine-free world.* http://lm.icbl.org
Photo caption: Landmine Action. The problem caused by anti-personnel mines. www.landmineaction.org

Arms Sellers
Grimmett R. *CRS Report for Congress. Conventional arms transfers to developing nations, 2000–2007.* 2008 October 23. Congressional Research Service. p.28. www.fas.org

Arms Buyers
Grimmett R. op. cit. p.43.

...the total annual budget
Shah A. The arms trade is big business. 2008 Nov 9. www.globalissues.org

54–55 Terrorism

Acts of Terrorism
Smith D. *The state of the world atlas.* New York: Penguin and London: Earthscan. 2008. pp.62-63.

Responses to Terrorism
Walker K. Terror law overkill? Mail Online. 2009 Feb 11. www.dailymail.co.uk
Terrorism Act 2006. www.opsi.gov.uk

56–57 UN Peacekeeping

UN Peacekeeping Operations Funding
...the total UN peacekeeping budget
United Nations Peacekeeping. www.un.org/Depts/dpko/dpko
Troop and police contributions [Accessed 2009 Aug.]
Fatalities by year.
2009 June fact sheet.

The Massacre of Srebrenica
Panos Pictures. www.panos.co.uk

58–59 Refugees, IDPs and Stateless
UNHCR Statistics. www.unhcr.org

Part 5: Discrimination

62–63 Religious Freedom & Persecution
US State Dept. *2008 Report on international religious freedom.* www.state.gov
International Coalition for Religious Freedom. *Religious freedom world report.* www.religiousfreedom.com [Accessed 2009 June.]

64–65 Minorities
Minority Rights Group International. *Peoples under threat 2009.* www.minoritygroups.org

66–67 Racism
Ending Racial Discrimination
United Nations Treaty Collection. http://treaties.un.org
Europe
France: Inter Press Service. 1998 June 22.
Romania
European Citizen for Minority Issues. *Intolerance in Romania.* Table 17. www.ecmi.de/emap
UK
Ministry of Justice. *Statistics on race and the criminal justice system 2006.* Cited by www.westsussex.gov.uk
MORI. *British views on immigration.* London: MORI. 2003.
India
US State Department. *Country reports on human rights practices 2008.* www.state.gov
Inequality in Romania
European Citizen for Minority Issues. *Intolerance in Romania.* Table 17. www.ecmi.de/emap
Inequality in USA
US National Urban League. *The state of Black America.* Cited by CNN. 2009 Mar 25. http://edition.cnn.com
The Office of Minority Health. www.omhrc.gov

68–69 Disabilities & Mental Health
Unequal Burden
...the WHO estimates
WHO. *Global burden of disease report 2004 update.* Part 3. Table 9. pp. 34-35 www.who.int

Disability Benefits
Mental Health Policies
Community Care
WHO. *Mental health atlas.* 2005. pp.15-19. www.who.int

70–71 Sexual Freedom
Legislation on Homosexuality
Ottosson D. *State censored homophobia: a world survey of laws prohibiting same-sex activity between consenting adults.* International Lesbian, Gay, Bisexual, Trans and Intersex Association. 2008. www.ilga.org
Iran
International Gay and Lesbian Human Rights Commission. *Annual report 2008.* www.iglhrc.org
Caribbean
Britain repeals laws banning homosexuality in Caribbean territories. 2001 Jan 5. www.GlobalGayz.com
Jones MA. Caribbean attitude towards homosexuality changing but violence toward LGBT people remains common. 2008 Oct 13. www.gayrights.change.org
Brazil
US State Department. Country reports on human rights practices 2008. www.state.gov
Increasing Recognition
Johnson R. Where is gay life legal? http://gaylife.about.com [Accessed 2009 July.]
Marriage and partnership rights for same-sex partners: country-by-country. www.ilga-europe.org [Accessed 2009 July.]
US states: Aunty Online. The Same-Sex Matrimonial Website www.auntyonline.com [Accessed 2009 July.]

Part 6 Women's Rights

74–75 Women's Civil Rights
Women's Rights
CIRI Human Rights Data Project http://ciri.binghamton.edu
Political rights: CIA world factbook www.cia.gov
Examples: US State Department. *Country reports on human rights 2008.* www.state.gov
Women and Poverty
US Census. American Community Survey.

Involvement in Civil Society
World Values Survey 2004. www.worldvaluessurvey.org

76–77 Domestic Violence
Women under Attack
Seager J. *The atlas of women in the world.* London: Earthscan and Berkeley: University of California Press, 4th ed. 2009. pp. 30-31.
United Nations INSTRAW http://www.un-instraw.org
Krug et al. *World report on violence and health.* Geneva: WHO. 2002. pp.90-91.
Ethiopia
García-Moreno et al. *WHO Multi-country study on women's health and domestic violence against women. Initial results on prevalence, health outcomes and women's responses.* Geneva: WHO. 2005.
Jordan
Jordan: Honour killings still tolerated. IRIN. 2007 Mar 11. www.irinnews.org
Jail for Jordan 'honour killing' BBC News. 2008 Dec 1. http://news.bbc.co.uk
What the UN says...
UNIFEM. *Facts and figures on violence against women.* www.unifem.org
Women's Views
Demographic Health Surveys www.measuredhs.com

78–79 Rape
Marital Rape in Law
Seager J. *The atlas of women in the world.* London: Earthscan and Berkeley: University of California Press, 4th ed. 2009. pp. 58–59.
Afghanistan: Afghan "anti-woman law changed". BBC News. 2009 July 8. www.bbc.co.uk
Rape
Seager J. op. cit. pp. 58–59.
UK: Williams R and Laville S. Police drive to set targets for rape investigations. 2009 April 15. www.guardian.co.uk
Rape in War Zones
Seager J. op. cit. pp. 100–01.
...one woman in five
UNFPA. *State of world population 2005. The promise of equality: gender equity, reproductive health and the Millennium Development Goals.* 2005. www.unfpa.org

80–81 Right to Choose
Access to Contraception
Seager J. *The atlas of women in the world*. London: Earthscan and Berkeley: University of California Press, 4th ed. 2009. p. 36. Data from: Sedgh G et al. *Women with an unmet need for contraception in developing countries and their reasons for not using a method.* Guttmacher Institute occasional report no. 37. 2007 June.

Legal Status of Abortion
Center for Reproductive Rights fact sheet 2008
http://reproductiverights.org

Unsafe Abortions
WHO. *Unsafe abortion: global and regional estimates of incidence of unsafe abortion and associated mortality in 2003.* Geneva: WHO. 2007. Table A3.1. www.who.int
Sedgh G et al. Induced abortion: rates and trends worldwide. *Lancet.* 2007. 370: 1338–45. Quoted by Guttmacher Institute. www.guttmacher.org

...26% of people
Isis International. www.isiswomen.org

...around 70,000 women
Singh S et al. *Abortion worldwide: a decade of uneven process.* New York: Guttmacher Institute. 2009.

82–83 Female Genital Mutilation
FGM Facts
...each year in Africa
...up to 140 million
WHO. Female genital mutilation. Fact sheet no. 241. 2008 May. www.who.int

Prevalence of Female Genital Mutilation
Seager J. *The atlas of women in the world*. London: Earthscan and Berkeley: University of California Press, 4th ed. 2009. p. 55. Based on data from a range of UN agencies.
Africa updated from: UNICEF. *State of the world's children 2009*. Figure 2.5. www.unicef.org

Legal Status of FGM
Rahman A & Toubia N. *Female genital mutilation: a guide to laws and policies worldwide*. London: Zed Books. 2000.
Seager J. *The atlas of women in the world*. London: Earthscan and Berkeley: University of California Press. 2009. p. 55.

84–85 Sex Slavery
Prosecution
...2 million children
...95% of women
US Department of State. *Trafficking in persons report 2009*. www.state.gov

Trafficking
Seager J. *The atlas of women in the world*. London: Earthscan and Berkeley: University of California Press, 4th ed. 2009. p. 56–57.
US Department of State. *Trafficking in persons report 2009*. www.state.gov

Part 7: Children's Rights

88–89 Child Labour
...over 101 million children
www.childinfo.org quoting UNICEF. *State of the world's children 2009.*

Bonded Labour
Zafar Mueen Nasir. *A rapid assessment of bonded labour in the carpet industry of Pakistan*. ILO Publications, 2004. www.ilo.org
www.rugmark.org

Type of Work
Working Children
Declining Incidence
Zafar Mueen Nasir. *A rapid assessment of bonded labour in the carpet industry of Pakistan*. ILO Publications. 2004. http://www.ilo.org

90–91 Child Soldiers
www.child-soldiers.org
United Nations Treaty Collection. http://treaties.un.org
Funeral for hero British soldier. 2009 July 31. Sky News. http://news.sky.com

Children of Violence
Child Soldiers, *Global report 2008*. www.child-soldiers.org

Ex-child soldiers speak
www.child-soldiers.org

92–93 Education
Primary Enrolment
UNICEF. Primary school enrolment and attendance. [Accessed 2009 Aug.] www.childinfo.org

Secondary Enrolment
UNICEF. Childinfo. Secondary school enrolment and attendance. [Accessed 2009 Aug.] www.childinfo.org

Not in School
UNICEF. Children out of school. www.childinfo.org [Accessed 2009 Aug.]

94–95 Child Mortality & Health
Child Deaths
World Bank. World Development Indicators infant and child mortality data. www.wri.org

...in 2007, 420,000
UNAIDS, WHO. *Aids epidemic update 2007*. www.unaids.org

...every 6 seconds
www.oxfam.org

Underweight Children
WHO. *World health report 2009*. p.13. www.who.int

Unequal Chance
WHO. *World health report 2009*. Table 8. Health inequities. www.who.int

Part 8: Country Profiles & World Data

98–113 Country Profiles
Amnesty International. *The state of the world's human rights 2008*. www.amnesty.org
BBC Country Profiles http://news.bbc.co.uk
Foreign & Commonwealth Office. *Annual report on human rights 2008*. www.fco.gov.uk
Human Rights Watch. *World report 2009*. www.hrw.org

114–121 World Data
Columns 1, 2, 4, 5 World Development Indicators www.wdi.org
Column 3 World Development Indicators 2007. Table 2.7. http://siteresources.worldbank.org
Column 6 WHO & UNICEF Joint Monitoring Programme www.wssinfo.org
Columns 7 & 8 UNICEF www.childinfo.org
Columns 9 & 10 UNHCR www.unhcr.org
Column 11 Reporters without Borders www.rsf.org
Column 12 Freedom House www.freedomhouse.org

Index

Index